GenTwenty's Guide to College Success

How to Ace More Than Your Finals

GenTwenty's Guide to College Success
How to Ace More Than Your Finals

EDITED BY NICOLE BOOZ

GenTwenty

2014

Cover art by Sarah Dilts
www.sarahdiltsdesign.com

First Printing: 2014

ISBN 978-0-692-31165-3

GenTwenty
1700 7th Ave Ste 116 #433
Seattle, WA 98101

www.gentwenty.com

Contents

College Facts.. 1

Introduction 3

Academics 5

Relationships 39

Self-Care...57

Student Finances 67

Planning For Your Future..77

TL; DR 94

About GenTwenty...97

References 99

Contributors

We would like to extend a warm and genuine thank you to the GenTwenty contributors whose thoughtful insights and experiences were instrumental in the creation of this book.

Anna Bailey
Molly Berg
Rachel Brandt
Marina Crouse
Natalee Desotell
Geralyn Dexter
Amanda Duncil
Janine Eccleston
Julie Eckardt
Emily Field
Tynisha Ferguson
Victoria Fry
Lindsey J. Gooden
Dana Johnson
Mara Johnson
Maggie McMillan
Madigan Naylor
Heather Newman
Abbygail Saddoy
Caroline Slavin
Rachael Tulipano

College Facts

1. 21 million students are attending college in the United States during the fall 2014 semester.

2. 18 million of these students are enrolled in undergraduate programs[1].

3. The average cost of tuition and fees for the 2013–2014 school year was $30,094 at private colleges, $8,893 for state residents at public colleges, and $22,203 for out-of-state students attending public universities[2].

4. One semester of textbooks will cost you approximately $550[3].

5. Employees with college degrees out earn employees without college degrees, averaging $45k compared to $30k, respectively[4].

6. Underemployment is rampant, with nearly half of college graduates holding positions that do not require a college degree[5].

7. Total student loan debt tops 1 trillion dollars. Over 11 percent of that number is 90 days delinquent.

8. The current average student loan debt is $27, 253[6].

Introduction

Some say college is the greatest time of your life. That's a lie. College is a great time in your life sure, but it is far from the best time you'll ever have. Do you really want to live in a world where the greatest things you will ever experience are behind you? I don't.

Through all of the great times and the hard times that college offered me, the most important lesson I learned when it comes to college success is:

You only get out of it what you put into it.

This holds true for most things. Your future career, your relationships, your current internship, and your job search are all dependent on the effort you are willing to put into them. This is a lesson that you will do well to remember sooner rather than later.

If you're reading this book, you already know that, whether you realize it or not. You also already know that you need to eat your vegetables, make your bed, and get to sleep at a reasonable time. You don't need us to tell you the basic things you need to accomplish each day.

In the following pages, we will share our been-there-done-that, tried-that-and-failed wisdom with you. Chances are you are still going to make the mistakes we did and you'll still learn from them. But what you will have that we didn't is the knowledge of where to go next.

You see, some of our lives are mapped out for us: Finish high school, go to college, find a job, have a family, have a mid-life crisis, find a new job, retire. The in-between times we are going through now are different from those that our parents experienced. So while your parents can support you, they don't know what to tell you.

But we do.

We're out here in the real world now, sometimes wishing we were back in our freshman dorm rooms with endless possibilities in front of us with nothing but the freedom to learn. College was good to us and it is going to be a great few years for you too, we just know it.

Nicole Booz

Editor-in-chief, GenTwenty

Academics

Your primary reason for going to college is learning. Your brain will be an information sponge over the next few years. You will be gaining relevant and eye-opening experiences. You will be challenging yourself in new ways and making lasting connections. But it's not as easy as it sounds. You'll be faced with a myriad of new pressures, sometimes from opposing parties. You will have more to do in a day than anyone can reasonably accomplish. You will need to learn how to make decisions that have your best interest in mind, how to manage your time, and how to navigate academia.

STEP 1: CHOOSING YOUR MAJOR
By Natalee Desotell

Choosing your major may be one of the most simultaneously exciting and anxiety-inducing aspects of college life. On the one hand, it's an opportunity to explore your interests and discover what you might want to do as a career someday. On the other hand, it is a big decision that will probably have a major (pun intended) impact on your life after school.

Some will insist that you're better off knowing exactly what you'd like to "do with your life" before you even start your first class. They'll tell you to declare a marketable major in your first semester and stick with it for the long haul. Others will assure you that your major doesn't lock you into a career; these people will say it's best to get a taste of many different avenues and decide late in your sophomore or even junior year where your true passion lies.

My advice falls somewhere in between.

First, get your generals out of the way. These are the classes you are required to take in order to graduate, such as basic math, literature, and science. Use this time (approximately your first year) to decide what areas of interest you want to pursue.

Use this first year wisely; talk to classmates about their majors, meet with program advisors, and take advantage of your professors' office hours. Ask questions, including the ones you might think are dumb, to find out more about all the options you have. Equally important is that you make good use of your time outside the classroom with internships or student organizations, which will help you pinpoint what really piques your interest.

By the time your second year rolls around, you should have at least a rough map of what the rest of your college career will look like. You are no longer directionless, but you are also keeping your options open to add a minor or even another major.

I suggest finding a major (or majors, I had three!) that will provide an equal amount of personal enjoyment and challenge. Striking a balance between so-called "hard skills" and "soft skills" is key to making the most of your education and being successful after graduation. Whether you choose to enter the workforce or apply to graduate school, your résumé will show that you are a well-rounded individual that any company or school would be lucky to have.

STEP 1A: FUELING YOUR PASSIONS (AND NOT YOUR PARENTS')
By Rachael Tulipano

Determining your personal concentrated area of study can be daunting. Glancing through your school's academic catalogue, there are many options to choose from.

Here's where you begin: it's important to consider every academic major. I know, I know, your parents are pushing you to follow their footsteps in biology, with a concentration in anatomy, so you can become a doctor someday, just like them. Whether that path appears interesting, or you feel swayed because your parents are footing your tuition bills each semester, please stop for a moment and consider your options.

College is about finding yourself. These are the four (more or less) consecutive years of your life where you are allowed, even encouraged, to make mistakes before transitioning into adulthood. Does ceramics sound like a fun art course? Have at it! Have you been itching to learn how to play the piano? Go for it.

My point is this: you're only going to (hopefully) attend college once. This is a brief chapter in your life where you are allowed to play around with your options. No, not every course may seem practical in the midst of building your résumé for a technical job. However, many of these courses will help you explore your passions, ultimately leading you to your dream major, or even career.

Studies demonstrate[7] that students who don't love their selected major will end up disliking college and ultimately hating their future job. What is the point of majoring in political science if you aren't politically affiliated in any way, shape, or form? You're absolutely right: nada. There's no reason to select a major that your parents see fit for you if you cannot imagine yourself in said field.

It's also important to remember that your major doesn't define you. According to New York Times journalist Jeffrey J. Selingo, your major may not matter as much as you think. His article, "The Choice"[8] discusses how most successful college graduates are those with interpersonal skills and critical thinking abilities.

If you find yourself in a major crisis, don't fret. You have four years to find your passions. Enroll in eccentric courses that stimulate your mind. Be an unconventional scholar, because chances are college is going to be far more memorable this way.

As for your parents? Encourage them to trust your judgment a bit more. This is your college experience. If they want to support you, kindly remind them you need to discover a major you're attracted to, all on your own.

STEP 2: CREATING YOUR *X* YEAR PLAN
By Nicole Booz

Not everyone will have a four year plan. You may have a two, three, or five year plan and that's perfectly fine. Throughout your college career, regardless of how many years it will take you to complete your degree, you need to have a plan.

First things first here, you should know all of your major or program's requirements. Familiarize yourself with the courses you need to take, their availability, and prerequisites. You should know all of your minor's requirements and how many elective credits you need to fill. Integrate any transfer or AP credits you may have.

Write all of this information down and keep it in an easily accessible folder (whether it is a physical folder in your dorm room or one on your desktop). You will be checking it at the beginning and end of every semester (sometimes in the middle, too) until the time you graduate.

Keep your plan flexible. You may fail a course and have to repeat it, you may not be able to get into a course because it was full, or the course may not be offered for the semester. Keeping note of these things and having a backup plan will ensure you are still able to graduate when you want to.

A note on college advisors: Do not rely on your advisor to make decisions for you or have your best interests in mind. Only you can determine your motivations and where you ultimately want to end up. It is your advisors job to know the requirements and conflicts - not what kind of coursework you specifically should be doing.

While creating your plan, be aware of the credit hour limitations and minimums that confine you. Check with your financial aid package to make sure you are maintaining the proper student stats (full-time or part-time) as a condition of your aid. Some grants or scholarships may require you to always be a full-time student (typically no less than 12 credit hours per semester) to continue to qualify.

Don't let other people's opinions sway you when it comes to determining which classes you want to take. We all perform best under different conditions and circumstances. Your best friend's distaste for a professor who only gives essay exams would not be helpful to you, someone who thrives with essay questions. If you are going to ask for someone else's opinion on a class or a professor, inquire about the class structure, exams, and teaching methods.

Plan your college career out for yourself – not for anyone else.

STEP 2A: CLASSES THAT WILL HELP YOU IN THE REAL WORLD (REGARDLESS OF YOUR MAJOR)
By Nicole Booz

According to Forbes[9] and The National Association of Colleges and Employers (NACE), employers are seeking out the skills and experiences they attribute to a valuable employee over individuals with specific degrees.

These skills are developed regardless of your major. They come from academic, professional, and personal experiences. The trick is to illustrate to your future employers that you have these skills.

Your jobs and internships you hold while pursuing a degree will help you build these skill sets. Below we have illustrated where you can learn them and how to apply them as relevant experience from a purely academic setting.

Skill	Class	Apply the Experience to Your Résumé
Teamwork	One that requires a semester-long group project	Describe how many people you worked with, your role in the group, and what you accomplished
Problem solving	Math, science or engineering courses	Briefly explain the problem you faced and how you solved it
Ability to plan, organize and prioritize	One that requires a semester-long project, thesis, or research paper	List the length of the project, the steps you took to ensure completion, and any methods you used to do so
Effective written and oral communication	Professional writing	Let your résumé and cover letter do the talking
Information gathering and processing	Any research-based class	Describe the project you worked on, how you gathered information, and how you processed it
Quantitative data analysis	Any research-based class, statistics	Explain what data you analyzed and with what programs
Technical knowledge	Courses within your major or field of interest that cover vocabulary and theory application	Use industry-relevant terms throughout your résumé and cover letter
Software programming	Introduction to programming	List the course, major projects completed, and languages used
Report creating and editing	Professional or technical writing; accounting or business, laboratory courses (based on your field of interest)	List types of reports you made and the programs, if any, you used to do so
Efficiency with influencing others	Marketing, communications; any course involving debate	Describe the campaigns you created and their outcomes, highlighting positive outcomes achieved

STEP 3: FINE-TUNING YOUR TIME MANAGEMENT SKILLS
By Rachel Brandt & Tynisha Ferguson

You're going to be very, very busy in college. The time you spend stressing over your packed schedule can be eliminated if you can learn to effectively manage your time early on. Try making some of these adjustments to organize your schedule:

1. **Avoid working in distracting environments**. If you are trying to knock out a full to-do list, then your dorm room is probably not the best environment to get things done. Create a dedicated workspace for yourself – somewhere you know you will be able to focus and complete the tasks at hand. Find yourself a quiet little corner in the campus library where you can go when you need to focus.

2. **Learn where your time is going**. Pick a day out of your already hectic schedule and track down everything you've done for that week and how much time you spent doing it. That way you will have a sense of what you're spending time on and what takes the most time for you to complete.

   Whether it's scrolling through 100 pages of Pinterest, stalking your friends on Facebook, or a Netflix binge, we are all guilty of wasting valuable time on useless stuff. Figure out your time-wasting triggers and avoid them when you are in a time crunch.

   Alternately, use them as incentives and reward yourself for accomplishing something. Make sure to build those rewards into your schedule. Twenty minutes on Facebook, six times a day adds up to two wasted hours a day. If that time is built into your schedule, then it's not a waste, it's a break to clear your mind and reset for your next obstacle.

3. **Prioritize and organize**. Use a planner or a calendar management system to keep track of the tasks you need

to get done. Prioritize your tasks according to importance and upcoming deadlines. Invest in a planner that suits your needs to help keep your to-do lists and deadlines organized.

4. **Stay focused when working from your computer**. We've all been there; you're working on an assignment on your computer, and the next thing you know, you're on Facebook, Twitter, Tumblr, Pinterest, and so on. Drop those habits and train yourself to stay focused on the task at hand and you will get hours of your time back.

5. **Stop multitasking**. Multitasking is the act of mentally jumping from one thing to another without actually completing anything; it leads to a lot of unfinished projects at the end of the day. Focusing on one item on your to-do list at a time means you can actually complete your work and give it your undivided attention. All that concentrated brain power is sure to improve both the quantity and the quality of the work that you are able to accomplish.

6. **Learn flexibility**. Look at what you need to do in a given time and divvy up the hours according to the size of the task. A good rule of thumb is to double your estimate for how long you think an assignment will take you. For example, if you think you can crank out a five page paper in two hours, give yourself four.

   If you finish early you can always add in quick tasks from your list to fill the time. You can also move things back if you run out of time. Be flexible as you get used to a more stringent self-inflicted schedule but also focus on getting better at estimating how long tasks will really take.

7. **Avoid being a pushover**. If a classmate or pal is asking you to help them with an assignment or to join a study group, and you know you know don't have time, say no. It's 100 percent okay to put yourself first. It's important to first have time for your own tasks before adding others'

responsibilities to your schedule; don't bite off more than you can chew.

If you have the discipline to use these tips to manage your time, you will not only feel like you have more hours each day, but you will be able to accomplish far more than your basic assignments for your classes (more on this in Step 6).

Additionally, if it feels overwhelming to form new time management habits, tackle them one at a time. If your problem is multitasking, form a new habit for that first before you track your entire day. If your biggest problem is saying "yes" to often, work on saying "no" first before you address your Pinterest problem.

STEP 3A: TIME MANAGEMENT APPS + WEBSITES[A]
By Amanda Duncil

Lift: This is a powerful, yet simple tool that allows you to track habits and keeps you accountable with a guilt-free environment. As you tally activities, it records progress so you can visually see your accomplishments. It also has an integrated social aspect to keep you motivated in your goals. Unfortunately, it's only available for iPhone and online. Android users can substitute with Google Keep; it won't be as cool or rewarding, but it gets the job done and syncs with Drive.

Pocket: If you're an Internet browsing junkie, you know the feeling of stumbling across an interesting read at the wrong moment. You could bookmark it or email it to yourself, but there's a good chance it'll be forgotten by the end of the day. This handy tool stores websites and articles so you can read them at a more opportune time. Pocket has cross-functionality with many popular apps. Optional browser extensions and in-app sharing gives

---

[a] This list of websites and the corresponding information were correct and up-to-date when this book was published.

you the ease of one-click saving, and the elegant magazine-styled design helps you visually connect with your headlines.

Nanny (Chrome) or **LeechBlock** (Firefox): When you know you should really focus on your work but can't resist the urge to browse social media—and being right at your fingertips makes it all the more tempting—turn on the Nanny or LeechBlock browser add-on to force yourself to behave. You define the parameters, including which sites to block and when. Both will let you set a specified time period to block access, or if you're afraid of going completely cold turkey, they allow you to set access to a site for a duration (ex: one hour max). It won't be as fun, but it'll cut off those pesky deterrents and let you get back to work uninterrupted.

Self-Control: Perfect for when you really need to focus and get your work done. It allows you to block out anything on the Internet that you find distracting for a set period of time. Instead of cutting your Internet access off completely, you can block and site that distracts you. Currently only available for Mac users.

Stay Focused: This Chrome extension is best for those who want to limit the time wasted on sites every day. If social media is distracting for you, install the app and give yourself 45 minutes a day to waste on Facebook or Twitter.

STEP 4: GETTING GOOD GRADES

Grades aren't the most important thing in college (we will get to that), but that doesn't mean you should neglect or ignore them. There are several components of making the Dean's List, and most of them are based on the effort you put forth.

STEP 4A: HOW TO TAKE REALLY GOOD NOTES
By Geralyn Dexter

Note taking. It's annoying and stressful, but much needed. Finding the balance between taking too many notes and making sure that you have the information that you need isn't always easy to do. What's important is finding a system that works for you. Here are some helpful tips that I've picked up in all of my years of schooling, no matter what note taking method you prefer.

1. **Don't worry about getting every word**. It's not possible. Instead of struggling to write everything you see on the PowerPoint or hear in a lecture, pick out the important parts and make sure you get that information. Names, dates, and definitions are just a few examples. Make sure you are able to connect the big ideas and concepts that are taught.

2. **Write what you don't know**. Don't waste your time writing down things that you already know. If you need to refresh your memory on something, section off a part of your paper and make it a "keywords" section and jot the word down there. Use your other course materials to refresh later. Make sure you get the information that you need on topics that you might need help with instead.

3. **Relate it to things that you already know**. If I'm having a difficult time wrapping my mind around a topic, I'll relate it to something that I understand or that reminds me of it. Using mnemonic devices or real world applications are a great way to conceptualize difficult things.

4. **Keep it simple**. Don't stress yourself out over taking notes! Keep it brief. Use bullet points. I like to use little hearts myself. Leave lines between points so you can add other things later or it doesn't look as crowded.

And last but not least: make sure you can read your own handwriting!

STEP 4B: THE ANATOMY OF A SYLLABUS
By Nicole Booz

The first thing you need to get your hands on for every single class at the beginning of every semester is your syllabus. It is going to be your number one tool for success during the course.

Every professor does his or her syllabus a little differently. It's rare that you will find two that look exactly the same, though most cover the same information, including: important due dates, course materials, grading criteria, extra resources, your professor and course information, your professor's exceptions, and learning objectives.

The syllabus is a roadmap for your class - it contains everything you need to do to earn top marks. You just need to learn how to use it to your advantage.

The reality of college is that your professors can't and won't be teaching you everything. Remember: professors and teaching assistants (TAs) are biased in the content they prefer to teach and how they want to teach it.

The professor who writes the syllabus is writing it from the perspective of what is important to them. They have their own preferences for what topics they prefer, how they like their papers written, etc. Figure out what your professor likes and do that.

Examine the course objectives and make sure to emphasize them in your papers and essay exam questions. Every time you get a chance to write out an answer, you have a chance to show that you can apply the knowledge you have.

For example, your course object may include learn how to write a proper lab report. Look over the samples your instructor provides and imitate it in your own work. However, do not under any circumstances copy it word for word. This is considered plagiarism and is not acceptable in any academic or professional setting.

Additionally, stick to the due dates. It is frustrating as a classmate and as a professor when someone continuously asks for extensions and to have dates moved. It disrupts the flow of the course and the professor's schedule. There are times when an extension is necessary (like if you were hospitalized) but 99 percent of the time, you need to respect the due dates.

When your professor makes an effort to help you as a student and make your life easier, thank them profusely. With the outrageous prices of college textbooks at $550 per semester[10], many professors will encourage you to use older versions of the book and provide you with corresponding page numbers to the new book's material. Thank them for that, it takes time and effort on their end for something they didn't have to do.

Finally, familiarize yourself with your professor's expectations. Most want you to show up, be ready, and engage in class. Do those things. Your professors are there to teach you and you are there to learn. If you make an effort to meet their expectations, they are more willing to make an effort to help you to learn, introduce you to valuable resources, and build a lasting connection with you. Make yourself worth their time and they will give it to you.

STEP 4C: PRACTICAL GRAMMAR:
A GUIDE TO AVOIDING COMMON MISTAKES
By Mara Johnson

A recent survey[11] conducted by Northeastern University shows that employers want graduates who can communicate effectively both orally and in writing. Here are some common grammatical errors to avoid in being a better speaker and writer.

1. They're/Their/There
   - "They're" = "They are"
     Ex: They're going to regret wearing stilettos to the beach.
   - "Their" is possessive
     Ex: Those girls are struggling to walk on the beach in their stilettos.
   - "There" refers to location or a particular point in a process
     Ex: Do you see those silly girls over there? Yeah, the ones wearing stilettos on the beach.

2. Affect/Effect
   - Trick: Alphabetically, "affect" comes before "effect." So, after you affect something, you get an effect.
   - "Affect" is most often a verb. Remember, affect equals action. They both begin with the letter "a"
     Ex: Superstitions don't affect my choices.
   - "Effect" is most often a noun and is the result of some action
     Ex: Superstition says that seeing a black cat has the unfortunate effect of bringing bad luck.

3. It's/Its
   - Trick: Say the sentence with "it is." If it sounds wrong, it probably is.
   - "It's" = "it is" or "it has"
     Ex: I'm so excited that it's finally fall!
   - "Its" is always possessive.

Ex: I love fall for its warm colors and sweater-friendly weather.

4. Then/Than
   - Trick: Use "than" when comparing things, and "then" in any other instance.
   - "Then" can have several meanings: At that time, next in the order of time, in addition to, etc.
     Ex: The kids brush their teeth, then they each breakfast.
   - "Than" is used when comparing things.
     Ex: The kids would rather eat sand than endure another bowl of Corn Flakes.

5. You're/Your
   - Trick: Say the sentence with "you are." If it sounds wrong, it probably is.
   - "You're" = "you are"
     Ex: You're not making a good impression by sending grammatically incorrect emails to the CEO.
   - "Your" is always possessive
     Ex: The CEO is so pleased with your grammar that you will promoted to President of Communications.

6. Loose/Lose
   - Trick: Use "lose" to refer to something that is lost. "Loose" is most often used in terms of fit/security.
   - "Lose" is a verb
     Ex: How could you lose my dog?
   - "Loose" is most often an adjective
     Ex: His collar was too loose, and he slipped right out!

7. To/Too/Two
   - Trick: Replace the word with "also." If it sounds wrong, it probably is.
   - "To" can have several meanings: a place/person/thing one moves toward, the direction of something, indicates relations, etc.

Ex: We should go to the mall before the party.
- "Too" means "also" or "to an excessive degree"
  Ex: Can I come too? I planned to wear my blue dress, but it's too small.
- "Two" is the number 2.
  Ex: Though, I can't decide between these other two dresses.

8. Me/Myself/I
   - Trick: Take the other noun out of the sentence and see if the sentence makes sense.
   - "Me" is an object (the thing acted upon or affected by the action)
     Ex: Paul ignored Jane and me when he saw us at the movies yesterday.
   - "Myself" is reflexive (you won't use it unless you've already mentioned yourself earlier in the sentence)
     Ex: I drove myself to the movies since Jane cancelled last-minute.
   - "I" is always the subject and performs the action.
     Ex: Jane and I went to the movies yesterday.

STEP 4D: BAD GRADES
By Nicole Booz

First of all, a bad grade is not the end of the world. In fact, a bad grade is worth its weight in gold because it teaches you a valuable life lesson: you aren't good at everything. It challenges you to try harder and find a new method that works for you.

Grades are often cited as a means of judging how well you follow instruction and your test-taking abilities rather than a true measure of intelligence. Sometimes your ability to follow instruction is more important than your intelligence. It's also true that most employers won't be looking at your transcripts, but that doesn't necessarily mean you want to walk around with an F next to your English class.

Follow these steps when you earn a grade that isn't up to your standards:

1. **Always do extra credit**. It doesn't matter what grades you are earning in the course for the semester. Do the extra credit that is offered.

2. **Talk to your professor or TA**. Most professors are understanding. They are people too, and have also struggled at some point during their career. Approach with caution and respect - your professor isn't out to get you. They will offer you feedback and resources to help you do better on your next assignment.

3. **Your grade is a reflection of the work you produced**. Ask yourself and be realistic - are you producing your best work 100 percent of the time? The answer is probably not. Forgoing a rough draft might work for you in some classes, but other courses will require extra time and attention. Give it to them.

4. **Do some calculating**. Whip out that syllabus and take into account the percentage your assignment is worth. Then calculate what grades you need to earn on the rest of assignments and exams in order to earn an A or a B. Incorporate the feedback from your professor into your new work.

5. **Examine the assignment and see where your weaknesses are**. It might be that a specific topic is escaping you, that you didn't follow the instructions properly, that you have minimal understanding of the material - it could be anything. Once you've identified your weakness, you can practice and devote more attention to studying it.

STEP 5: BUILDING RELATIONSHIPS WITH YOUR PROFESSORS

By Natalee Desotell

Unless you're at a small university where classes are cozy and professors actually learn their students' names, it may be difficult to take full advantage of one of your most important assets for surviving college and succeeding afterwards: your professors.

Through guidance or shining letters of recommendation, professors can help you jump the hurdles to get into graduate school or to get your foot in the door of your first job after college. If you want to get the most out of your years in school, building a positive relationship with one or two of your professors each semester ought to be on your to-do list.

Here are a few of the tactics I used to stand out from the rest of the class.

1. **Be a good student**. No, you don't need to receive perfect grades to be a good student. In my opinion, being a good student means that you're making a genuine effort to learn the material. First, show them that you're taking your studies seriously by introducing yourself to them in the first week. I usually also include why I've chosen their class and what I'm looking forward to most.

   Next, read the syllabus thoroughly and follow their rules to a T. They know that you've made it to college and therefore they know you can read, so most professors have little tolerance for students who fail to familiarize themselves with the rules of the classroom. Further, you should always go to class–extra points if you sit up front so they always see that you're there.

2. **Know that they want to talk to you**. Students often fail to meet with their professors because they feel like they'll bother the professor them or that they won't have anything to say to the professor. But presumably, professors took their jobs because they wanted to help students and because they

like to talk. For these reasons, it's safe to assume that they probably appreciate it when you show up to their office. That's not to say there aren't some crotchety old professors who seem to hate their students. Not everyone can be Mr. Feeny.

3. **Arrive prepared**. When you're planning to talk with a professor, it's best to be prepared. If you have a question on an assignment, make sure you've actually attempted the assignment and completed the necessary reading and prep work.

   This one is hopefully obvious, but I can't even count the number of times I've heard my classmates ask questions that could have been easily answered by doing the assigned reading. Don't embarrass yourself by making that mistake.

   Next, if you're interested in discussing their research, take some time to skim at least one of their publications and their CV. They'll be impressed if you're familiar with their colleagues and their research. In my experience, professors always appreciate it when a student is prepared for the conversation.

4. **Keep in touch**. This may be the most important step in the process. It's very helpful to them if you stay in touch, especially if you plan to request a letter of recommendation a few years down the road.

   I start by sending a thoughtful thank you to a professor after grades have been posted (no one likes a brown noser) to show my appreciation for taking time to chat with me. Later, I contact them every once in a while to remind them that I exist and to show that I'm still interested in the subject.

   Sometimes I include links to interesting articles that might be relevant for their class. Other times, I send a note to let them know what I'm doing and how their advising helped me get there. Don't go overboard, though; a professor isn't likely to write a great letter of recommendation for their stalker. One note about every six to nine months is plenty to keep you fresh in their mind.

Getting to know your professors is one of the most important networking opportunities that you have in college. Follow these steps and you'll find that knowing your professors will open many doors for you, inside and outside the classroom.

10 WAYS COLLEGE PROFESSORS AND HIGH SCHOOL TEACHERS ARE DIFFERENT

	High School Teachers...	**College Professors...**
Expertise	are knowledgeable on their subjects but are primarily trained in teaching methods.	are experts in their fields and hold advanced degrees.
Teaching Methods	will provide you information as you will be tested, draw direct connections for you. They follow a teaching schedule that parallels your textbook.	each has his or her own style. They include additional information that you won't be tested on in their lectures. They are focused on larger concepts and how to apply them.
Expectations	will monitor your progress and will reach out when you seem to be struggling. They expect that you will be responsive to their efforts.	expect you to make connections yourself, to think critically and apply your knowledge. If you need help, it is your responsibility to reach out to them.
Reminders	will remind you daily of due dates	will rarely remind you of due dates.
Assignments	give in-class assignments (otherwise known as "busywork"). They check for both correctness and completeness.	rarely give in-class assignments. The assignments that are assigned are checked for correctness.
Class Attendance	require attendance and keep track of it.	occasionally require your attendance, but most often leave it unrecorded.
Exams	often regurgitate material covered in class on exams. Sometimes the material is covered verbatim as it was taught.	require you to think critically and apply your knowledge in a variety of ways on exams, but most often with essay questions.
Note taking	assist you by writing supplemental notes for you to indicate important material.	often lecture non-stop and take minimal time to indicate important details.
Additional help	are usually available between all classes, as they stay in one environment all day.	are only available during assigned office hours (some may be responsive to email).
Responsibility	take responsibility for your success by giving you the tools you need and helping you build the skills you need to receive high marks.	expect for you to already have the tools and skills you need to learn and apply what you've learned. They take minimal responsibility for your grades and efforts.

STEP 6: THINGS YOU NEED TO WORRY ABOUT INSTEAD OF YOUR GPA
By Dana Johnson

Although grades are important, they alone won't land you a dream job. You need to supplement your academic endeavors with tangible work experience, and doing so means you'll need to leave the library once in a while.

Grades certainly play a factor when employers consider potential job candidates, there are many factors that can increase your likelihood of being hired. It's wise to aim for a minimum 3.0 GPA, but you shouldn't let your grades alone determine how you spend your time while in college. Be proactive (and realistic) about planning for the future, and work hard to score relevant opportunities early on.

Instead of focusing so intently on your grades, here are a few other things to spend your time doing:

1. **Seek out relevant experiences**. There are countless opportunities to get experience in your field, if you're willing to take advantage of them. Many student run organizations also offer valuable work experiences. An aspiring magazine editor could work for the school newspaper or edit newsletters for the English department. Someone interested in broadcasting could take a weekly shift at the university radio station.

   Even local organizations can offer great experiences that will help to build your résumé. You can gain experience in everything from grant writing to tree trimming simply by seeking out local opportunities. Although these opportunities rarely have monetary benefits, they can work as critical stepping stones on your future career path. For opportunities off campus, check with the local Chamber of Commerce.

2. **Begin to think about the future**. Don't fool yourself into thinking you have "plenty of time" to find a job. You should begin formulating your career goals as soon as you sign your

major. You'll need to start searching for employment opportunities long before you graduate, and the application process can be daunting. Research the types of companies you might want to work for, familiarize yourself with positions in your field, and apply for relevant internships. Create a LinkedIn account and begin networking with professionals.

The more prepared you are for the job hunt, the less overwhelming it will be when the time to send out your résumé inevitably comes, and seeking out relevant opportunities might lead to contacts you can utilize in the future. Not to mention, employers are seeking self-motivated, forward thinking individuals. Being strategic in your job search will allow you to practice these skills and grab the attention of employers.

3. **Have fun.** Yes, college is full of seemingly unbearable stress, botched relationships, psychotic roommates, grimy apartments, and moments of debilitating loneliness (or is that just me?), but it's also likely one of the most unique and life changing experiences you'll have. Enjoy it. Once college is over, you probably won't have the luxury of sleeping in every Tuesday, of walking across campus in the sunshine, or of spending breaks napping in the courtyard next to Brown Hall. Enjoy these things while you can, even if it means you don't get all your reading done today.

If you ever find yourself wondering if the C you got in your Early Childhood Development course is truly going to have a profound negative impact on your career as an accountant, it isn't. Employers seem to understand this. It's okay if your grades slip in some areas, as long as you make up for it by bulking up your résumé with work experiences, extracurricular involvement, and internship credit. Remember to stay motivated, practice a positive attitude, and formulate specific goals for the future.

Like with all aspects of life, the key is to find a healthy balance. Don't let yourself get overwhelmed from the pressure of maintaining a 4.0. Just remember to work hard, have fun, and be happy.

STEP 6A: HOW TO STAND OUT AS A COLLEGE STUDENT
By Dana Johnson

Despite feeling like a special snowflake, you're actually one of hundreds of thousands of students who are just like you. Some of your classes may be small, but others will reach into the triple digits and it's important that you stand out - in a good way.

1. **Participate in class discussion**. Although you can usually hide in the crowd in larger lecture halls, as you get more credit hours under your belt, you'll find your class sizes dwindling. While your professors will expect you to be engaged and alert, many of your classmates will attempt to dodge every question that comes from the front of the room.

   Stand out from the crowd by engaging the class in conversation. Give your opinion on the topic you just covered. Ask a question if something is unclear to you. Being fearless and confident in your classes won't just get the attention of your classmates; it'll look good to your professor too.

2. **Come prepared**. This tip is so simple, yet so many students fail to do it. Take a few extra minutes each day to truly prepare for class. Print off your course material, mark the chapter you'll be reviewing that day, grab a calculator if you know you'll need one, and of course, read the textbook.

   If you're prepared in your courses, others will notice. What's more, you'll be more engaged in class, which will save you time from having to catch up later. While the rest of your classmates are scrounging around in their backpacks for lost notes, you can enjoy a nice study break in the student center.

3. **Work hard, then play hard**. Trust me, it's possible (tricky, but possible) to do both. College will be some of the most demanding years of your life, but they'll also be some of the most fun. The key is to find a good balance between the two.

   Spend your early weeknights and weekend days in the library, so that you can enjoy karaoke night on Fridays, or a couple of house parties on Saturdays. Most students tend to fall toward one extreme or the other. Many party too hard and let their grades slip, while others spend every waking moment in the library without a break for fun. Don't let yourself get too obsessed with either end of the spectrum.

4. **Utilize your resources**. Your university has endless resources that are there for you to explore, so utilize them! Join a dance team, workout in the fitness center, ask questions of your librarians, and always take advantage of being surrounded by academic professionals. Your professors are there to help you.

   Not sure if you want to pursue an MFA or go straight into the workforce? Talk it over with your instructor to get some advice. Looking for a part-time job? Check openings in your department of study. So many students only utilize their university for academics, but there is so much more that your school has to offer.

You can truly stand out from other students by seeking out the resources that mean the most to you.

STEP 7: STUDYING ABROAD – SHOULD YOU OR SHOULDN'T YOU?

By Madigan Naylor

We've all had that one friend that goes abroad and comes back claiming that "it was the time of my life" or "it changed me forever." I used to roll my eyes when they said this and continued to tell me about their crazy times and wild experiences—until I spent a semester living abroad myself.

While these statements may be cliché, they have every bit of truth behind them. Not only did studying abroad change my life, but it prepared me for real life and I believe you should do it while you still can.

Living in a completely unfamiliar place forces you to take a look at yourself and focus on what you want and who you want to be. You also meet people that will help you get there.

While abroad, I made friends with a group of girls that became some of the most cherished friends I will ever have. They helped me become who I am today and who I am going to be in the future. Everyone who goes abroad shares these sentiments. When you're dropped into a new, strange place, you find people that you bond with because they are going through the same things you are and you figure it all out together.

Not only do you learn so much about yourself and the world around you while studying abroad, but it also prepares you for real life situations that can occur in the future. When studying abroad, you learn to go with the flow when things unexpectedly don't go your way. Trains may not run on schedule, your passport and wallet may get stolen, and you may have to sleep in a bunk next to an old man in a hostel that speaks a language you've never heard in your life (and who snores like a freight train)... but you learn to deal with it and move on.

Being abroad, no matter where you go, teaches you how to communicate with people from all different walks of life. You open your mind to new things, and you become a more mature person because of this.

Your trip looks good on your résumé. Employers see that you have tried new things and have learned how to deal with many different kinds of people. I got a job because I bonded with my new boss over our conversation about our travels. Our conversation left a lasting impression on her. And frankly, having it on your résumé helps you look well-rounded.

STEP 8: MAKING THE MOST OF SUMMER AND WINTER BREAKS
By Mara Johnson

It can be tempting to want to use your breaks for relaxing and catching up with friends, but for the most part, that isn't the best use of your time away from campus.

1. **Network**. It takes more than finishing your degree to actually accomplish your career goals. Networking is one of the most beneficial things you can do to advance within your industry (you know this is important because we will be mentioning it a lot). Depending on where you are in your college career, you might think it's too early to start, but good impressions and connections are long-lasting.

   Think about it this way: If you act now, you have the opportunity to gain insider knowledge, connect with experienced professionals in your desired industry, and foster a relationship with them over a one to four year period. By the time you finish school, you will have a better grasp of how the industry actually functions in the real world, and you significantly increase the odds of getting a job because the key players will already know your name.

2. **Take part in a short-term internship or shadow**. Participating in an internship or shadowing gives you the perfect

opportunity to test drive a career, and ensure that you actually want to end up where your path is leading you. If you haven't yet decided on a career pursuit, or you've got the ever-common cold feet, an internship or shadowing allows you to sample what lies ahead without actually having to commit to it.

Much like networking, if you're able to make a good impression, internships in particular can be extended, and there is always the possibility of receiving a job offer after graduation. If you can't find an appropriate internship or shadow opportunity - volunteer! Not many organizations will turn away a volunteer, and you still get the experience you are after.

3. **Go on a volunteer or mission trip**. Not only is it a great way to travel, but you will get to learn about another culture and provide much-needed assistance along the way. If you can't study abroad for an entire semester, this is a great alternative to adding valuable travel experience to your résumé.

4. **Find scholarships and grants**. College is expensive. Luckily, there are countless scholarships and grants available, and they are particularly great because unlike student loans, they don't have to be paid back. That's right, it's free money.

Searching for scholarships and grants can be time consuming, but since you're on a break, you probably have some time to spare, and can find one that will make it worthwhile.

Unfortunately, many people miss these opportunities because they make the false assumption that they aren't "scholarship material," but there are scholarships available for things you would probably never imagine: being left-handed, being short or tall, being a skateboarder, or a great marbles player. The possibilities are virtually endless, and the less debt you can graduate with, the better.

5. **Decompress and have some fun**. Joline Godfrey, financial educator and CEO of Independent Means Inc., said it best, "All work and no play doesn't just make Jill and Jack dull, it kills the potential of discovery, mastery, and openness to change and flexibility, and it hinders innovation and invention."

   A lot of people have the tendency to forget that having fun is a legitimately important factor in maintaining a good attitude about the work they're doing. With studying for tests, reading assignments, club meetings, and whatever else is on your plate, it is easy to feel like you're too busy to look away from your work, but you have to make room for fun every now and then.

   Otherwise, you could find yourself feeling like you never get to do the things you want to do, instead of always doing what you have to do, and that can lead to being miserable. If you're someone who struggles with prioritizing fun, make it a reward. Set a firm goal of how much work you will accomplish, and when you hit that mark, take a break, and treat yourself because you've earned it.

Your breaks between semesters give you time off from academics, but that doesn't mean you need to be complacent and hole up with Netflix (although, you most certainly can). If you want to add other experiences to your time in college, a break is a great time to give it your undivided attention.

STEP 9: EXPERIENCING ACADEMIC PROBATION
By Lindsey J. Gooden

Before you shake your head and skip this step, remember that academic probation can happen to anyone. It is crucial to recognize that it is not a reflection of your intelligence and understand that it merely means you need to reevaluate your priorities and your methods.

When you're in the process of going to school, keeping everything balanced can be a major hassle. Sometimes the stress and pressure become too much and you find yourself in hot water.

One day everything is kind of "meh" and the next you're getting a letter stating you've been put on academic probation[12]. Now you have holds on your college records, the possibility of being suspended, counselors and advisors to meet with, and the overwhelming sense of "dear God, how did this happen?"

Try to keep calm and proceed as follows:

1. **Cry**. Just do it. You know you want to and I can guarantee you'll feel a hell of a lot better afterwards. It might not solve anything, but crying will let out all the feels you're holding on to.

2. **Figure out what happened**. Time to be honest with yourself, chances are you'll have to meet with an advisor and answer this question for them so you might as well figure it out for yourself first. Maybe your party habits got the best of you, you took on too much at one time, your mental health took a turn for the worst, or something serious went down in the family. Whatever it was, just be straight up with yourself and identify what it was that threw off your groove. Ideally you can confront that problem first to ensure it won't come creeping back next semester to wreak even more havoc upon your GPA.

3. **Forgive yourself**. This is a difficult step. It'll take time to stop scolding yourself, too. You'll feel sick about what your family would think and you'll compare yourself to friends and peers. Forgiveness doesn't have to happen right away, though. Let the idea enter your mind so you can at least try to get closer to coming to terms with what has happened.

4. **Sharing is caring**. This is also a difficult step. Now's the time where you take a deep breath, meet up with a friend for

coffee, and say, "Guess what happened to me the other day." You might feel embarrassed or ashamed, but it's okay! Only tell those who really matter to you because chances are that if you care about them, they care about you too.

They can also act as a major source of inspiration and support. Tell those people what the upcoming classes you'll be taking are; they'll ask how your classes are going now. Maybe they'll even propose study dates with you. Have your significant other ask what you've been learning about. If the people you love show an interest in what you're doing, you'll likely pay more attention to what you're doing.

5. **What do you really love**? You'll probably have one or two required classes that you should take care of. But then... be selfish. Find a class or two that really interests you, one that you'll be excited about attending every week. Bread and Circuses: Entertainment and Spectacle in the Roman Empire? Homoeroticism in Popular Media? From Dracula to Twilight: the Role of the Vampire in Literature? Gang Culture and Youth Violence?

   It doesn't have to be a class you need or even one that will benefit you in the future. If it's something you're interested in, you'll be naturally encouraged to pay attention and try hard. Doing your homework isn't so much of a chore when it requires you to study something you've always been interested in. And who knows? That favorite class could ignite the spark that'll get you feeling like a kick-ass student again.

6. **And then, take it easy**. You've likely just had a bit of a rough time with some aspect of life (AKA what threw you off course in the first place). Expecting yourself to be running at full throttle again is too much. Take it all one step at a time and don't put too much pressure on yourself. You could try taking one less class for your next semester or try to limit how many hours a week you spend at work. Think of it as recovery mode—you're being kind to yourself so you can get back to being your usual, fabulous self.

You may feel foolish or incompetent at times, but try to remember that you've done so much hard work to get to where you are. Just because you feel like you can't write a paper anymore or study effectively doesn't mean you're done for. If you could do it before, you can do it again.

And don't let the small victories go by unnoticed. Celebrate your first good quiz grade! Show your lover the comments on your successful paper! Whatever you were dealing with that got you into the academic probation status is behind you. You've dealt with the problem head on and have worked hard. Even the smallest of successes deserve a reward.

Oh, and once you've gotten yourself out of academic probation status... let there be cake.

STEP 9A: 10 SIGNS YOU'RE IN TROUBLE
By Nicole Booz

If you've failed an exam or an assignment, it's obvious that you need to do some reevaluating and fast. There are subtler signs pointing in the direction of trouble that you should pay attention to.

1. You're extremely homesick.
2. You spend more time procrastinating than you spend doing actual work.
3. You find yourself skipping more classes than you are attending.
4. You have no motivation or excitement to learn new material.
5. An outside source (friends, family members, or a professor) has expressed concern.
6. You have trouble sleeping and maintaining patterns.
7. You push off your own needs to cater to the needs of others.
8. Your attitude towards everything, including socializing, is in the "I don't care" realm.

9. Dread is a common feeling when you are on your way to class or work.
10. You spend hours going over the same material without comprehending anything.

More likely than not, one or more of these signs will present themselves to you during your college years. Heed them - they are often symptoms of a larger problem at hand.

It's OK to feel overwhelmed, it's OK to not know what to do next, it's OK to not understand material. It's not OK to let yourself ignore the symptoms and warning signs.

Relationships

Relationships are a foundation of college. Arguably, there is nothing more important than the relationships you form while you are pursuing higher education. Make an effort to befriend every person you meet. If there is one secret to the real world, it's that who you know makes all the difference.

STEP 10: SETTING GROUND RULES: LIVING WITH ROOMMATES
By Marina Crouse & Maggie McMillan

You may or may not get to choose your roommates in college. In either case, there several things to take into consideration before and during the time you live together.

First, and some people may argue on this, but I would advise not to live with a best friend. I know, you're thinking, "but I love my friend, we would never fight," think again. Living with someone is totally different from hanging out with them casually. Unless you know your friend is a slob, a neat freak, a party animal, a loner, etc. and you're completely ready to accept their qualities, don't do it.

Then again, living with a stranger, can be hard to get used to. I suggest as soon as you move in, get to know each other. This way you can learn about them, their likes and dislikes, and give each other feedback if there are things you disagree with. By doing this you'll know early on whether you'll enjoy living with this person. If you don't discuss these things and set boundaries then, when your roommates start to do something you don't like, it can end in a fight and with you living awkwardly in silence trying to avoid one another.

Alternatively, you and your roommate don't have to be joined at the hip. It's okay to have separate friends and not hang out with each other all the time on campus. It doesn't mean you don't like each other. Space is good, especially when you're already seeing this person every day.

Remember, communication is key. Don't expect your roommate to know what you're thinking. If they did something you don't like – moved something, used something, said something hurtful – just talk to them about it, but in a mature, adult way. Nobody likes to be badgered or accused. Don't play the passive aggressive card either. Be upfront and honest about what's bothering you without being accusatory or rude.

Create your own roommate contract that highlights the differences of opinion you may have when it comes to your personal belongings and your shared space. It's important to address issues before they occur. For example, the two of you may agree that borrowing clothes is acceptable only if you ask permission and approved the article of clothing. Talk about issues like dirty dishes, shared chores (like trash duty), and overall ways to approach touchy subjects so neither of you feels uncomfortable when the time comes to bring up a specific incident.

Additionally, respect your roommate for her decisions and choices, and ask that she do the same. Create an environment where you know you can go to her with a question or concern without worrying about defensiveness or passive aggressive reactions.

And finally, don't hold grudges. It's important to be able to let things go. You roommate leaves her dirty dishes in the sink for too long? It's okay to be upset about it, but address the situation with a calm conversation. Maybe she's overwhelmed with work and forgot about the cereal bowl that was left on the counter yesterday. And if she just doesn't clean up after herself, remind her about shared spaces, contribution, and the roommate contract. Chances are, somewhere along the line you've done something to upset her, so remember that no one is perfect.

STEP 10A: MAKING THE BEST OF YOUR COLLEGE LIVING SITUATION
By Dana Johnson

College is a time full of adjustments, and your college living situation is no different. Whether you're moving into a dorm for the first time or signing your third apartment lease, it takes a lot of effort to get used to new roommates, particularly if you've never met them before.

We've all heard the tips for getting along with new faces: Set ground rules, make a chore chart, and compromise, compromise, compromise. This advice is all well and good, but after living with a total of seven different people throughout my three and a half years in college, I've learned that there is a lot more to the puzzle than just getting along with your roommates.

Ultimately, the key to having a healthy living situation isn't about correcting any else's habits. It's about approaching all challenges as potential for your own personal growth.

1. **Learn to adjust**. Unless you plan to stay in college forever, your living situation is only temporary. Although it's important to treat your new dorm room or townhouse like it's your home, remember that you're not back in high school. There's no one older and wiser to remind you to lock the door when you leave or pick your towel up off the bathroom floor. If you weren't already, college is the time when you'll need to become independent and self-sufficient.

   Little habits that seem insignificant to you, may create a lot of irritation for your roommate(s). Just the same, sharing a house with someone with different cleaning habits may create unnecessary tension. Remember to be self-aware. Every action, no matter how small, is going to have an effect on those closest to you.

2. **Find creative solutions**. Everyone is different, and has different habits. For example, when I study, I need complete quiet. The hum of a television in the next room, music echoing out of the headphones of the person next to me, or excessive yelling from a party down the street are all annoyances that keep me from being productive.

   Regardless, the majority of my roommates throughout college were able to study while blasting music or watching TV. Because I was the unique one, I made a point to do all my studying in the library or in campus study rooms. If I needed to be productive, I knew that going home was not an option for me, and I adjusted to this fact quickly. Even though it was a minor nuisance to have to wake up early on Saturdays, get dressed, and drive to the library (instead of doing my homework in bed), it was a solution that allowed me to get my work done. I couldn't ask my roommates to stop watching TV, but I could certainly make an adjustment in how and where I did my own work.

3. **Remember, the only person you can change is yourself**. No matter how many conversations you have with your roommates, and no matter how many chore wheels you create, the only person's behavior you have control to change is your own.

   You get irritated when your roommate blasts Eminem in the middle of the afternoon? Make it a point to be out of the room at that time. You can't stand a messy kitchen? Buy a set of dishware just for you, so you know you'll always have a clean set to use. Trying to change those around you may only result in tension. Change your own behavior, adjust, and you will be significantly more likely to have a healthy living situation.

4. **Understand compromise early on**. Learning to live with your peers, no matter how unique or different they may be from you, is a great learning opportunity. By living with others, you can test your patience, become more self-aware, and learn how to adjust your own behaviors to suit challenging situations. Compromising with your roommates is a great way to solve conflict, but there's no guarantee that they will commit to change, even if you do. Instead of focusing solely on the behaviors of others, focus on yourself and your own personal growth.

Always remember, college is challenging, but it's a truly unique privilege that only lasts a few years. Make the most of it, and appreciate every moment, even if that means dragging yourself out of bed to drive to the library on Saturday mornings.

STEP 10B: 5 TIPS FOR CONFLICT MANAGEMENT
By Nicole Booz

Living with roommates gives you a chance to practice your conflict management skills. Though we may hope for a perfect world, that's simply not the case.

1. **Do not be passive aggressive**. The thing about conflict is that, for the most part, the two (or more) parties involved do not understand where the other is coming from. Your passive aggressive moves aren't sending the signals you think they are sending. Be upfront and clear about your feelings.

2. **Set up a time to talk - in a neutral setting**. If your dorm room or apartment is a source of tension, talk to your roommate somewhere else. Being outside of the toxic environment will help you think more clearly.

3. **Talk about how their actions make you feel**. While you can't force them to change their actions, you can let them know that you find it distracting to study with the TV on or you have trouble sleeping with the light on. Don't ignore your feelings, but make sure you share them in a healthy way before you bottle them up for too long.

4. **Create compromise**. You aren't going to always get your way, and this is the perfect time to learn how to compromise. Reach a solution that you both can live with.

5. **Show respect**. You both have feelings, and regardless of how the other party feels, you need to respect it, even if you don't understand it.

Note: You should never stay in a living situation if it is harmful to either your physical or mental health. If you have repeatedly extended an olive branch to an unresponsive roommate only to be threatened or ignored, do everything you can to remove yourself from the situation.

STEP 11: MANAGING YOUR LONG-DISTANCE RELATIONSHIPS
By Caroline Slavin

There's no getting around it. Long-distance relationships are hard work, whether you and your significant other are going to different universities in the same state or are an ocean away due to study abroad. The great thing about long-distance relationships, though, is that they force couples to trust and communicate with each other. While these are both key to any successful relationship, they are crucial during long-distance. Anything less than open and honest communication creates painfully obvious roadblocks from the start.

Manage your long distance relationship by being clear and up-front about what you need from your significant other. Since you're not in the same place physically, you need to be on the same page in other ways. If you want a text every morning before you go to class, speak up! If you need to Skype with each other at least three times a week, let them know! Body language and passive signals are unreadable in a long-distance relationship, so you have to use your words to let the other person know what you're thinking and feeling.

Because physical communication and intimacy are both scarce in long distance relationships, get creative when it comes to being physical with your partner. While in-person visits are always top priority, they're not always practical. Sending snail mail letters and care packages can be a tangible way to show you care.

Of course, modern technology allows for visual physical intimacy with the click of a button. Taking advantage of video calls and texting pictures in this way is a great way to tide you over between visits. It goes without saying, though, that caution should always be exercised here. First check your local, state, and national laws and make sure that you and your partner are both legally of age before you send and receive anything explicit.

Second, even if you completely trust your partner with sensitive photos or videos, things can happen. Things can always end up in the wrong hands. Make sure you're 100 percent comfortable with everyone (including future employers and your grandma) seeing your pictures, otherwise make sure that nothing identifiable is in the frame.

If both you and your partner are willing to put in the work to really trust each other and communicate effectively, distance will only make your relationship stronger. Give each other the space to grow as individuals and trust that they will be eager to share their experiences and thoughts with you at the end of the day.

Be willing to put aside time to talk on Skype, but be willing to trust when your partner says they're knee-deep in a chemistry project and will call you later. Long-distance is hard, but as long as you are both willing to put in the effort, it will be just one chapter in an ultimately stronger relationship.

STEP 12: HOW TO NETWORK WITH ANYONE
By Amanda Duncil

Networking opportunities are everywhere, but it is up to you to initiate the conversation.

1. **First, you need to redefine your idea of networking**. Networking can appear as an insincere way of obtaining contacts who are worth something to you or your career. You might be inclined to veer from cultivating your contact pool if you feel disingenuous or fake while doing it. Ditch the notion that networking equals making friends in order to get something in return and think of it more in terms of social networking. Reaching out to like-minded students that you are genuinely interested in keeping contact with will foster stronger relationships. You won't expect any special favors and you'll both be more inclined to help each other should the need ever arise.

2. **Talk to everyone**. By far, the most difficult part of building a network is meeting people outside of your immediate circle. Joining a student group or club is a great way to meet people with similar interests. Just be yourself and make yourself available.

3. **Don't forget the internet**! You might want to write-off Facebook or Twitter as creating fake relationships, but social media is a great tool for getting to know people outside of your immediate area.

   They also allow you to stay in touch with existing contacts much easier than a business card will. There's no doubt that it's more convenient to pass along information (links, articles, videos) but it's also easier to talk to someone this way if face-to-face interaction make you freeze up.

4. **Stay in touch**. Forming new relationships is only half of the battle. Remember to keep them active by periodically engaging with your contacts on a regular basis. Conversations shouldn't be strictly business, either. Pass along any information they could possibly use, see how they are doing and maybe ask if they want to grab a bite and chat.

It's important to remember that while a vast network is a great resource to have, it isn't a magical solution to getting anything you want. They are relationships that need to be cultivated, otherwise they won't grow and benefit you in the future. We will cover more on networking in Step 27.

STEP 12A: 10 PEOPLE YOU SHOULD MAKE CONNECTIONS WITH
By Julie Eckardt

Networking is an essential skill. College is the best time to hone and perfect that skill. Here are 10 key people you should get to know while you're working on your degree:

1. **Your advisor**. While you'll probably only formally meet with this person a couple times a semester to discuss signing up for classes (and often only when you have a problem), but the better they know you, the better off you'll be. Not that they would intentionally hurt your chances of getting into a class, but if they know what your interests are and the things you are interested in, they can point you in the right direction and offer suggestions that can make your college experience much more rewarding and fulfilling.

2. **The people in your department's main office**. Again, these are probably not people you'll see often, but when you do need them, you really need them. These are the people who will collect any degree requirements (such as a portfolio) and will answer any questions you have. Being friendly will make your visits less awkward and uncomfortable for all involved.

3. **Your upper-level professors**, especially those who teach subjects you're really interested in. In line with the importance of networking while you're in school is the importance of finding a mentor figure. Get to know them by asking about their story, their professional paths, and their advice for you, someone who is interested in their field.

4. **Students in your year and major**. Let's be real, you're going to be stuck with these folks for a while, you might as well get to know them a little. I always found it helpful to make at least one friend in each class you're in. Not necessarily a friend in the "let's hang out all the time outside of class and be BFF" kind of way, but more in the ally kind of way. Just so you have at least one person in the class to talk to, partner up with, compare notes with, and make snide comments to. And you'll likely have more classes with them as you both continue your education, so you might as well have people you can share your grievances with through the years. You never know, maybe the friendship will flourish beyond sitting next to each other in class.

5. **Your Resident Assistant (RA) while you're living in the dorms**. For the most part, RAs are super chill people who just want their whole floor to get along and plan fun things for you all to do together. But, the second that someone is making drama, they will crack down on them and make it stop. Don't be that person. No one on your floor likes that person anyway. Just keep the peace on your floor and everyone will be happier.

6. **The head of your department** (or at least know who they are and who any other higher-ups are). This person (and their committee) are the decision-makers for your whole department. They decide what emphases continue to exist and how many classes that teach a certain subject are open every semester. While you probably won't meet them (unless they're one of your professors), it's just as important to know who they are so you know who's in charge.

7. **Professors you want to take classes from**. If a class is in high demand (which many upper level classes are) and the number of seats is limited, you can quickly find yourself in a hard place if all you need to graduate is that class and you can't get it. While many professors are open to squeezing a couple more people in, they'll be much more open to squeezing you in if you make yourself known to them (or are at least polite and professional in the email you send them begging to let you in). Making friends with them will also open up conversations about other classes they are teaching so you know what to plan for in your next few semesters.

8. **Anyone in the counseling center**. College is hard; just all around hard. You'll reach multiple low points where you'll just want to give up and leave. Those in the counseling center can help you. I went to counseling for about a semester my sophomore year and it helped me through a really rough patch. Keep in mind, too, that this is one of the only times that counseling is free, so it's better to take advantage of it now while you can.

9. **A local**. When you're dropped into a college town that you know nothing about, the sooner you can get to know all the good spots in the city, the better. You'll quickly find that many of things are word-of-mouth among students (such as good bar spots for particular moods, the best place to get groceries, the best student apartments, etc.), but the little details are left unsaid. Making friends with someone who is from the area can help fill in the gaps and show you where all the best spots are for everything, especially those things beyond the typical student radius.

10. **An upperclassmen in your major**. Making friends with an upperclassman in your major is almost a requirement for your sanity. This friend can warn you about assignments in a certain class, advise against certain professors, and understands the pain and stress of your major. Upperclassmen will guide you through the dark. They've been there; they will help you.

Bonus: Know who your university president is and, if possible, introduce yourself and greet them whenever you see them. While knowing them might now give you any sway in anything (but that's not the point), it's cool knowing that your school's president knows who you are, especially if you're at a big state university.

People are an essential part of your college experience and collaboration with like-minded people with help you greatly. Even if your relationship is nothing more than friendly interactions as you pass each other in the hall, the more people know of you, the better off you're going to be when you need to call in a favor.

STEP 12B: SMALL TALK 101

By Victoria Fry & Heather Newman

No one genuinely enjoys small talk, but it is still a necessary part of networking and getting to know people. It's unfortunate, but true nonetheless. If you weren't born with the gift of conversation, allow us to help you out:

1. **Prepare ahead of time**. Before you head out to that gathering of yours, prepare in advance of topics to talk about. This might sound silly, but all I'm saying is to keep up with the news! Everyone has some form of news cross his or her path throughout the week. Catch up on the latest celebrity scandals and what's being debated about in the newspapers. You'll be glad you did when you can fill that conversation with your own opinions about what's going on in the world.

2. **Give a little to get a little**. When trying to have a small side conversation with someone, you can briefly bring up something that you like. Let them know the latest book you've read or a movie you've seen. Maybe they just read or watched the same thing, or something similar. By suggesting something personal that you like, they may feel comfortable enough to share something that they like as well.

3. **Let it be all about them**. While we can all only hope that we get stuck with the one person who loves to talk about themselves and fill the silence, this is not always the case. By subtly asking a person questions and urging them to talk about themselves, you'll be flying through your short conversation! Ask your companion how their day was or about their job. Generic questions will do the trick! Now is the time to become a great listener.

4. **And then, decipher what you have in common**. Whether it's a book you both love or a class you've both taken, use it as a starting point. Chances are you have a good bit to say about whatever it is. Listen carefully to what they respond, because ...

5. **... it's your best shot at crafting a conversation that flows**. Take note of specific facts they reveal, places they mention, people they know, and use them to branch off into other areas. If something intrigues you, ask for more info. If something confuses you, ask for clarification. If and when they turn the focus on you, try and reference something they said within your answer. It keeps it from sounding like a rehearsed speech and turns the conversation into a Lego project rather than a tennis match.

6. **Don't be so anxious that you forget this is ideally a two-person effort**. If you're too focused on remembering and executing your pre-prepared conversation topics, you might miss an important nuance of the conversation. Even worse, the person you're talking to might feel you're not paying attention to them. Take a deep breath and listen carefully. The best clues emerge from the conversation you're having, not the one droning on in your head.

7. **When your conversation winds down**, whether it's because someone is calling you over or the presentation is about to start, don't walk away without having introduced yourself, especially if this seems like a connection you want to maintain. At the very least, it's polite to exchange names, if only so you can say, "Nice talking to you, Sarah!" It's a little extra touch that's not only courteous but memorable–especially if you remember their name next time you see them.

STEP 13: GREEK LIFE
By Anna Bailey

We're aware that there are many aspects of Greek Life, but we aren't going to go into them (sorry). The biggest thing you need to consider is if Greek Life is the life for you. Because there are a lot of stereotypes surrounding sorority life, we are going to break down what it looks like on the inside, and how you can use your membership to your future benefit.

It is not until someone is actually a part of a sorority that they realize that the things these women learn are important. Not only are they a part of an organization that prides themselves on the connection between women and the enhancement of feminism, but also the few years spent inside the Greek organization teaches you how to be a functional member of society after college.

So, although it is difficult to understand how it works on the inside when you are standing outside, here are a few features of a sorority that can help build your résumé and make you a better person – in the professional and personal sense.

1. **Leadership opportunities**. There are many different positions that can be held within a sorority's chapter and, though they vary slightly from organization to organization, each position helps you learn as a leader and understand your place among other leaders.

2. **Time management**. Between having to balance school, work, and spending time with your beloved sisters, it is no wonder that sorority girls know how to cram a full day's worth of activities into a few hours and still get them done well.

3. **Lasting friendships and networking opportunities**. A sorority girl knows from the moment she gets her bid that she will have a hundred-plus girls who will let her crash on their couch even three years after college. She will have girls who will bring her soup when she feels like she is lying on her deathbed, and she will have those girls long after the tassel has been turned. The misconception is that a sorority is just "paying for your friends," but it is about finding respect from girls who love you unconditionally.

Going Greek may be right for you, but it may be completely wrong. You won't know until you check it out, so if it's something you think you might be interested in, check it out.

STEP 14: DEALING WITH HOMESICKNESSES
By Abbygail Saddoy

Even though most won't admit it, being homesick in college is quite common. On top of school work, extracurricular activities and the new responsibilities of adulthood, college students tend to feel homesick no matter how far they have traveled from home. To feel homesick is completely natural. Thankfully, there is more than one way to cure your ache.

1. **Go out on the town**. If your school is in or near the city, check out what there is to do! You're there for a few years, so you might as well get to know your surroundings. Chances are, there will be plenty of events to attend and new sights to take in. You might even learn a thing or two outside the class-room. If and when your friends and family come to visit you, you'll know the best places to hit. You'll be able to share things that make the city unique. Everyone loves to explore!

2. **Try new things**. As a college student, you're bound to meet people with different interests. Try a new activity; it could turn into a new interest that will lead you to a new group of friends. Try that new Vietnamese restaurant down the street or that new comedy club around the corner. When you do go back home, you can share your new interests with your loved ones and can get them excited about it too.

3. **Get physical**. Get the endorphins flowing! Besides the gym, try walking the long way to class, baking without an electric mixer, or painting your room a new color. Try cleaning your room or reorganizing your space for a fresh outlook. Being physical can clear your head and might even bring you new ideas.

4. **Call home**. Make the time to talk to your loved ones, whether it's through texting, Facebook, FaceTime, or Skype. Something simple as picking up the phone can relieve your homesickness in a matter of seconds.

Other ways to cope with homesickness are to read a book for fun, hop on Netflix to binge on your favorite movies, get in the spirit at a sporting event, get silly at karaoke night, write down your feelings in a journal, or volunteer your time for a cause that's important to you.

Just remember that being homesick is completely normal. You're in an environment you're not familiar with and it's overwhelming: that's okay. Remember to make the best out of it knowing your friends and family are there to support you. Change is scary, but it's worth it and you will grow so much from the experience.

Self-Care

For most of us, college is the first time we are really on our own. It's up to you to wake up on time for class, stay motivated, feed yourself, do your homework, hit the gym, and manage your social calendar. These things seem simple, but we will be the first to tell you that they are not. It is really a balancing act and you will, at times, find yourself completely overwhelmed. Set a routine early on in your college career that helps keep you balanced.

STEP 15: MASTER THE DINING HALL

By Julie Eckardt

When living on campus, you're rarely left with many eating options. After all, you can only get so far with a just a fridge, a microwave, and a hot pot, especially when your only access to a full kitchen is shared with the other 400 or more residents in your dorm. Thus, on the one day of the week that you don't order a pizza or Chinese food, you must navigate your final choice: the dorm cafeteria.

College cafeterias, though each is going to be slightly different, follow the same lines: reminiscent of your high school cafeteria, but usually with a wider variety of food options and staffed by students. Some try to spruce their cafeterias up to try to make it look more like a coffee shop or a Panera, but when it comes down to it, it's still your school's cafeteria and there isn't much more to do there but eat, debrief about the night before with your friends, and gear up before heading off to class.

Still, they're an integral part of anyone's college education and can often be hard to tackle, at least without knowing the best course of action, anyway. Here are five directions to get you started:

1. **Know what's always there**. Most cafeterias have different stations to satisfy anyone's appetite. After breakfast comes and goes, these stations usually include a grill so you can get your burger and fries on, a pizza station (usually the cheapest option if you're in a pinch), an Asian fusion station for all your teriyaki and generic stir-fry needs, a salad bar, and a station where they serve the closest thing to a home-cooked meal you're going to see until you go home for Thanksgiving.

   Each has its pros and cons, and your preference for each will usually reflect what time of the semester it is. You'll probably eat healthier early in the semester, dedicating yourself to working on yourself as well as your schoolwork, but as the first round of tests and term papers come screaming through, you'll find yourself reaching for the burgers (my dorm cafeteria made a killer grilled cheese that became my saving grace during hard times) and pizza more than the salads. And that's just fine.

2. **Know what's good**. While most of the stations won't provide much variety beyond one day having sausage pizza and the next day only having pepperoni, the home-cooked station will change. Some meals will much better than others, but it's important to know what to keep an eye out for.

My cafeteria had this mac and cheese that only got wheeled out about once every other month, but it was the perfect amount of gooey, creamy, and cheesy that hit the spot every time. Their M&M cookies, too, though rarely seen, were always delicious. You'll learn pretty quickly what's good, what's tolerable, and what's outright disgusting.

3. **Know what's gross**. In a college cafeteria, there's often a fine line between what's edible, what's gross, and what will probably make you sick. While cafeterias are, in fact, highly regulated (public schools especially really don't want to be sued if they can avoid it) and clean, there is the occasional dish that your stomach will not agree with. Not only should you always be stocked with Tums, but you should also make a note every time you need them.

At my school, they made this chicken quesadilla, and I don't know what was in it, but it made all of us sick. Then there are dishes that are just plain gross. Even when I worked there, there was this one dish I was serving that my manager actually had me throw out because everyone was complaining that it was disgusting and inedible. There will be times where the chefs just aren't nailing it. It's important to remember those dishes that didn't make the cut and never eat them again.

4. **Know the hours**. While most of the workers at cafeterias are students, there are many, such as the actual chefs and supervisors that are working this as their regular nine to five job. Thus, the hours at a cafeteria can get a little screwy and good to remember so you don't end up without dinner because you were too sucked into your studying. Many schools, in addition to the cafeterias, have convenience store-type markets that are open later hours, but these markets often only offer microwave meals that can leave you still hungry and unsatisfied. So memorize the hours and you'll be set!

5. **Lastly, remember that most of the employees are students, just like you**. While you should never ever be rude to people who are serving you, it's important to extend this courtesy to those working in college cafeterias. Trust me, they hate their job and have much better things to do (like study) that they'd rather be doing than cleaning up the tray of food that you made into a swamp and glopping mystery meat onto your plate.

   Working in a kitchen is hot, miserable, and does not pay well. Add the stress of being a full-time student and the humiliation of having to deal with fellow students (including people you have classes with) and you have a recipe for shot egos and dampened spirits. It's not a good time. To help them get through their shift easier, be patient, kind, and please (please) pick up after yourself. It makes everyone's day easier if you nicely take your tray to its designated drop area. Thank you in advance.

All in all, a college cafeteria isn't that different from a mall food court or what you experienced before you hit higher education. There are still the same plastic and forever wet trays (that do make excellent sleds, by the way), the same mystery concoctions behind greasy sneeze guards, and the same members-only ability to buy food. The only difference is that this is going to be a consistent source of food for you as long as you're living on campus, so it's in your best interest to learn ropes as quickly as you can. Hopefully it won't be too terrible.

STEP 16: DON'T SKIP THE GYM
By Maggie McMillan

College is probably the only time you'll have access to a state of the art gym for free (okay - not really for free, it's included in your tuition, but that's just even more reason to go).

If you aren't quite sure where to start, don't worry - this is the first time many of your classmates will be going to a real gym as well, so you're bound to run into someone who also has no idea what machine does what.

On that note, go with a buddy. If you're walking into a gym alone for the first time, it can be a little overwhelming; all the new people and strange machines can make your feel isolated and confused. If you're alone, you may start feeling too overwhelmed and find yourself making excuses not to go. Also, they may know the answers to questions you may have about different machines or workouts. But mostly, going with a buddy can keep you on track. With someone to push you or by making a set schedule, you'll be more likely to go.

Don't compare yourself to other gym-goers. The gym hosts all types of people – many of whom may look like they've been working out for years – but don't let this discourage you. Remember not to compare yourself to others. You are a different person and we all have different body types. But going to the gym isn't just about how you look, it's also about how you feel. It's about the fact that you've decided you want to feel good and be healthy. When you decide to stop focusing on those around you and focus on yourself, you'll notice your anxieties starting to slip away.

Do some research. Check up on the machines they have at your gym and do some research on them as well. By knowing the machines and a little about how they work, you'll be a little more at ease when you begin using them. Check for group a group fitness class schedule. These classes, like Zumba® or kickboxing are a great alternative to endless treadmill miles.

The most important thing is that you are getting some kind of physical exercise. Bodies were made to move and after spending hours sitting in class, yours will be grateful for the opportunity.

STEP 17: TAKING CARE OF YOUR MENTAL HEALTH
By Lindsey J. Gooden

Anyone who's attended college can tell you that it can be an incredibly stressful environment. Not all stress is bad, though. In healthy amounts[13], stress can provide adrenaline rushes, boost your immune system, or help your body recuperate after a particularly intense workout.

However, it's important that you're able to distinguish the healthy stress from its more negative counterpart. If you frequently find yourself falling victim to the negative stuff, it's time to figure out how to make yourself feel better.

Exercise (see Step 16) is one of the best ways to get rid of unwanted stress, not to mention it has countless other health benefits. A quick biology review: exercise releases endorphins[14], a chemical responsible for making you feel happy. By committing to go swimming twice a week or running through the park on Mondays and Wednesdays, you're triggering the release of your body's endorphins, thus making you feel happier and less preoccupied with stress. Yoga and mindfulness meditation are also two good exercises for alleviating stress and keeping your mind in check, especially if the elliptical isn't your thing.

One of the smallest and simplest things you can do to reduce day-to-day college stress is to keep an up-to-date calendar or planner. These only work though if you actually use them. We recommend that once a week—Sunday evening may be best—sit down and go through an overview of what you can expect in the week to come. Look at your class syllabuses and schedules and write down any upcoming assignments, quizzes, presentations, workshops, or exams. This will take about ten minutes a week and make keeping track of everything a breeze.

Another rather simple method of alleviating school stress is to talk to someone. Sitting down with a friend and ranting for ten minutes about how ridiculous your chemistry professor's expectations are for the class will make you feel so much better. It might not get any of your homework done and it probably won't change your professor's attitude, but vocalizing your frustrations will help you feel better. It's a lot like crying; none of your problems really get fixed, but you end up feeling less of that internal stress and pressure.

If talking to friends isn't enough though and you feel yourself becoming overwhelmed by responsibilities, seek out more help. Schedule an appointment with your advisor, find a guidance counselor, or look into visiting your school's mental health services. There's absolutely nothing wrong with admitting that you feel too much pressure. In fact, more power to you for being honest with yourself and knowing your limits.

And though it may be important to stay on top of your college responsibilities, it's crucial to stake out a bit of time for yourself. Don't forget to indulge in your favorite hobbies and make some time to spend with friends and family. Remember that the most effective way to take care of college stress is to be sure that you're taking care of yourself.

STEP 18: ALCOHOL AWARENESS AND MYTHS
By Julie Eckardt

Lessons involving alcohol are usually (and unfortunately) learned the hard way. Many times, we go into our first few experiences with little knowledge of what to expect or of what our limits are.

Not only is safety potentially an issue, but there are a number of myths associated with drinking that should be busted for the class.

Myth 1: Men and women process alcohol the same way.

If you as a girl are trying to keep up with your male friends at a party, then you are going to be feeling the effects a lot faster. Not only do men typically weigh more, but they have higher quantities of the stomach enzyme called alcohol dehydrogenase, which breaks down the alcohol so not as much enters the blood, according to a TIME Magazine article[15].

More alcohol in the blood means a higher blood alcohol content (BAC). If your BAC gets too high, you run the risk of liver damage, alcohol poisoning, or even death if you push it too far.

Myth 2: BAC and Tolerance are the same thing.

Some people are more experienced than others. This usually means that they can drink more than less experienced drinkers before feeling like they got hit by a truck. This is tolerance.

However, three shots in an hour is three shots in an hour whether this is the first time you've drank or the fiftieth. For a woman who weighs about 150 pounds, three shots (drinks) in an hour puts your BAC is .092, which is above the legal limit in most states, according to Washington State University Alcohol and Drug Counseling, Assessment, and Prevention Services[16]. And that number is the same whether you are a seasoned drinker or not.

Just because you may not be feeling the effects (and may be encouraged to drink more until you do), doesn't mean that your blood and liver aren't suffering the consequences.

Myth 3: Mixing alcohol and energy drinks isn't as bad as people say it is.

Between the occasional Vodka Red Bull or Four Loko, you've probably felt the weird effects of the low of alcohol, which is a depressant[17], and the high of the energy drink–and the crash when things go sour.

According to drugfree.org[18], a study recently came out that participants that had a drink that contained both alcohol and an energy drink had impaired judgment, but weren't as aware that they had it.

Being unaware of your impaired judgment is extremely dangerous, as you may feel okay to drive or do things that you normally wouldn't do were you more aware of your impairment.

Myth 4: It's okay to come back to a drink you've left if you're with people you trust.

Rule number one of partying: once you put a drink down, it's dead to you, even if you are with people you trust. As if it isn't scary enough that one in four women get raped while they're attending college, 90% of victims[19] actually knew their attacker. While it shouldn't be your responsibility to protect yourself from offenders and people should just be kind to one another, be safe while you're out, especially where alcohol is involved. Everyone's judgment is impaired and things can go south really quickly.

All in all, where alcohol is involved, be safe and be smart. Alcohol can be a fun way to hang out with people, but just keep in mind the potential dangers associated with it.

Student Finances

Because college is (probably) the first time you are living on your own, it's also (probably) the first time you've ever really needed to manage your own money. Take the time to get into good financial habits now - your future self will thank you tremendously. College is an expensive venture. From tuition to housing to transportation costs to miscellaneous living expenses, the list is endless. If you learn to budget and spend wisely early on, you'll graduate far ahead of your peers and will have more flexibility in your career options.

STEP 19: COLLEGE MONEY TRAPS AND HOW TO AVOID THEM
By Nicole Booz

College is expensive, but we have a few tricks up our sleeves for reducing the cost of some of higher education's biggest expenses.

1. **Tuition**. It varies, but with the average cost of tuition being $30k per year, you might want to consider other options before jumping straight into a four year program. You can complete many elective and core credits at your local community college for only a fraction of that price tag. Check with the credit requirements of the schools you would like to attend before making any hasty decisions.

2. **Textbooks**. One of the biggest money traps of a college education is textbooks. Rather than spending $600 per semester on textbooks at your campus bookstore, look into alternatives for cheaper textbooks. Wait until the semester has started to see if you actually need a textbook. Sometimes, professors will list a textbook as required but never use it. Sign up for an Amazon Student account (www.amazon.com/student) for free two-day shipping, access to reduced price textbook rentals and used copies.

> ### Textbook Resources
>
> **For rentals**: chegg.com, bookrenter.com, amazon.com, campusbookrentals.com
> **For purchasing used**: amazon.com, bigwords.com, your school's book exchange
> **For free**: your school library (limited copies available, check early), gutenberg.org

3. **Your dining plan (and food in general)**. Unless you are planning to eat every single meal in the dining hall, you probably don't need the most expensive dining plan. Choose one that allows for flexibility as dining halls are not always convenient during the day. A flexible dining plan will allow you

to grab lunch at the student union instead of trekking back to the dining hall midday. If you have a busy schedule, it may be better for you to keep a mini-fridge well stocked and only visit the dining hall occasionally, meaning you only need the cheapest dining plan available.

4. **Coffee**, otherwise known as the lifeblood of college students, can break your budget if you aren't careful. Your campus library or student union may offer free coffee to students. If they don't, skip the lattes and macchiatos at the coffee bar in favor of black or lightly sweetened coffee. You'll save $2-3 per cup, easy.

5. **College-branded clothing**. Your schools logo, hoodie, and mascot are cute but spending $40 on one sweatshirt is not. Wait until there is a sale or check out stores near your campus for much cheaper apparel. Additionally, join some clubs or attend events around campus. Often time they give away clothing and other items for free. By the time you graduate, you'll have so many t-shirts you won't know what to do with them. Additionally, if you drop in at student orientations or programs around campus, you'll get free notebooks, pens, and pencils. Who cares what they look like if you didn't have to spend a dime on them.

> **Pro-tip:** No matter where you are shopping, always ask if they offer a student discount. Many stores give a discount of 5-20 percent off if you flash your student ID.

6. **Transportation**. You might already have a car, but there are still costs associated with keeping it with you at school. Not only is there gas and insurance to pay for, but in most cases you will be paying a few hundred dollars for a parking spot each semester. If you want another form of transportation other than your own two feet, familiarize yourself with your campus' bus system or invest in a bike.

7. **Housing**. Look into off-campus housing options rather than on-campus or student branded housing. With a roommate or two, living off-campus in a regular apartment building can save you a few hundred dollars a month. Even without a roommate, an off campus studio apartment can be a better value rent-wise than having multiple roommates on campus.

STEP 19A: DORM ROOM ESSENTIALS AND SCHOOL SUPPLIES
By Nicole Booz

Your dorm room is your temporary home and should be cozy, but don't let yourself be overwhelmed by cute branding and new patterns each semester. The things you buy your freshman year can easily last all four years of college (trust us - you really don't need a new comforter every year).

Your resident association has probably provided you with a list for the basic things you need to bring, but in our experience, these are the things they forget to mention that you will actually need:

- At least one good lamp
- Mattress topper (pay attention to what size bed your school provides)
- A few extra pillows and extra blanket
- First aid kit
- Shower caddy and shower shoes
- Bulletin board or whiteboard
- Storage options and containers
- A basic printer with extra ink
- Eating utensils
- Dish soap
- Hand sanitizer
- Disinfecting wipes
- Laundry detergent

STEP 20: USING YOUR STUDENT LOANS TO AVOID DEBT
By Janine Eccleston

It's really no secret that there are tons of twenty-somethings with tens of thousands of dollars in student loans. New grads become overwhelmed when it comes time to pay for the education they borrowed for years earlier. Unfortunately, post-secondary education isn't cheap, most students graduate with over $27,000 in student loan debt[20]. This five-figure sum is a huge burden to take on when trying to land your first job. While you can't erase the past, you can help yourself mitigate this potential burden. Here are four simple tips that will show you how to responsibly spend your student loans and minimize the amount you take on.

1. **Create a budget**. Identifying what your monthly expenses will be gives you a good idea as to how much money you need to be bringing in each month. Include your rent, groceries, utilities, transportation costs, and other expenses that occur each and every month. If you don't plan on working enough to cover your monthly expenses, your student loans will have to supplement your income.

   This isn't a bad thing, but knowing how much you need to cover those expenses will help you minimize the amount of borrowed dollars you will need to fund your lifestyle. Creating a budget will help you do this. (See Step 20).

2. **Supplement your income with a part-time job**. Getting a part time job is vital to ensuring your student loans are minimized. Whether you are picking up a couple of shifts a week at a coffee shop, or babysitting for a few hours every month, all of this supplementary income will help you in the future.

   Part-time income could be the difference between having $30,000 of debt when you graduate or $20,000 of debt. While working extra hours may not be the most ideal with your grueling college schedule, you'll appreciate it down the line.

3. **Pay for your needs and cut the wants**. Traveling to exotic locations, going out for dinner with your friends every week, and picking up your daily latte are all wants – and they are all excellent ways to waste your student loan money. Give yourself a reasonable weekly/monthly allowance and say no to those "wants" that don't fit within your budget.

While student loans can help supplement your lifestyle when you're in school, it's important to remember that it's not free money — you will have to pay it back someday. But if you're smart about it, you will be able to lessen your student loan debt and your future-self will thank you for it.

Remember, you don't have to accept your total financial aid package either. If you can supplement your income and tuition payments in other ways, that's better than taking out additional money you'll have to pay back someday.

STEP 21: BUILDING YOUR COLLEGE BUDGET
By Janine Eccleston

College is fun, but it can be overwhelming with a lot of classes, exams, and assignments. From a financial standpoint, many people can feel overwhelmed with how to balance their course load and their bank account. By following this simple guide you will be on the road to financial success:

1. **Define your income**. Figure out all the sources of incoming money: it could include a paycheck from your part-time job, leftover student loan money, a supplemental allowance from your parents, or even scholarships are all part of your income. Your income is the first line of your budget and it should be your after-tax (or net) income. You don't get to keep all your income, due to taxes, so you shouldn't include it all in your budget. If you are utilizing student loans we would suggest taking the amount you receive for the semester and dividing

it by the number of months in the semester. Give yourself that amount each month to pay your bills and keep the rest in a savings account, that way you won't be tempted to spend it all in one go.

2. **Cover your needs**. Your needs are defined as the things you require to survive. Food, clothing, shelter are all things you require to keep yourself afloat. Shopping, movies, and lavish dinners out do not constitute needs.

   Since you're a student you will also need to make sure you are covering your tuition and textbooks. Pay your tuition with the money in your savings first and then turn to student loans. There is no reason you need to max out the amount you borrow. Remember - the more you borrow from the bank or the government the more you will have to pay back after you graduate.

3. **Include savings**. This is one of if not the most important steps to building your budget. Savings needs to be part of your budget; it's imperative.
   Monthly contributions, even small ones, can make a huge difference down the road. Even when you are a student, try to sock away some money each month. $25 or $50 a month may not seem like a lot, but if you continue to do this over the course of a four-year degree you will end up with thousands of dollars put away for your future.

4. **Now for your wants**. After taking into account your needs and including savings in your budget, you can then allocate the rest of your money to your wants. By taking care of your needs and savings you can spend the rest of your money guilt-free on things you want and enjoy.

   As a student you will have to be frugal with your disposable income. You can't buy everything you see and you certainly can't go out for dinner every night. But if you work hard, and pay yourself first, there is no reason you can't go for a beer with friends every now and again.

5. **Make it flexible**. Budgets have to be flexible. Depending on your situation your budget can and will change. Having a buffer in your budget allows you to adapt to different situations without going into to debt. As a student your income may also be variable in which case having a buffer will help you in month where you make less than expected. Remember to track what you are spending so that you can compare what you budgeted to what you actually spent.

By following these simple steps you will be able to build a budget that covers all your needs, ensuring you are saving for your goals and future and still have fun in your twenties.

STEP 22: UNDERSTANDING THE BASICS OF CREDIT AND HOW TO BUILD YOURS
By Nicole Booz

Credit cards are notoriously synonymous for financial trouble, but you need to recognize that your credit history is imperative for a happy financial future.

First of all, there are a few things you need to know about credit. Credit is a reflection of how financially responsible you are. If you are able to borrow money, repay it on time, and in full without having a delinquent account or declaring bankruptcy. Having good credit is going to be a necessary thing in your life if you ever want to purchase a home or a car. (Note: Even if you can purchase things outright, including a million dollar home, it's still best to be prepared and have a good credit score).

There are three types of credit: revolving credit, open credit, and installment credit.

Revolving credit is your credit card, you have a fixed amount you are allowed to "borrow," but it has to be paid back or you are charged interest.

Installment credit is a borrowed amount that has a fixed monthly repayment schedule. Your student loans fall under this, as do a home buying loans and auto loans.

Open credit must be repaid in full every month. Chances are you will only encounter this with special types of credit cards (including business cards), where you have no limit, but must pay back the amount in full or else you are charged outrageous interest.

Having student loans will start your credit history if you have no previous experience with credit cards, but they are only one piece of the puzzle.

Opening your first credit card can be intimidating, especially with all of the fine print. But don't be too discouraged, here are our tips for opening your first credit card:

1. Choose a student card or a credit card affiliated with your bank.
2. If you aren't approved for one of those, start with a store credit card. A smart move is to make it one that you don't frequent, otherwise you are putting yourself at risk for spending more than you can afford.
3. Remember that a low limit is a good limit. If it's not available to be spent, you won't be able to spend it.
4. Consult your parents or other trusted adults. They've probably been around the block a time or two and may have even had to rebuild their credit after a few poor financial decisions. They won't be too keen to see you in that situation, so they will offer you sound advice on what card is best for you.
5. Shop around. Find a card that fits your lifestyle. Cash back might be good for you, but a miles card might also be a good idea. Do your research - there is no one-size-fits-all answer here.

The non-negotiable rules of credit cards that you always need to follow:

1. Don't open more than one while you are in college.

2. As a rule of thumb to keep your spending in check, never put more on your credit card than you have in cash.
3. Avoid carrying a balance on your card.
4. Always pay your bill on time. (Pro-tip: If the due date doesn't work with your paycheck schedule, call the company and see if they can change it to a date that works better for you).
5. Never go over your limit. There are often heavy fees and higher interest when you spend more than you are allowed to. Don't rely on your card to be denied either, it's better for the credit card company if you aren't spending wisely. They make more money that way.

Other things you need to know:

1. A late payment negatively affects your credit score.
2. If you are going to miss a payment, schedule it ahead of time. If your payment is late, contact a customer service representative. Most companies have a one-time late payment forgiveness policy and you should take advantage of it if you are ever in the situation.
3. Travel hacking with credit cards is on the rise, but don't worry about that while you are in college. Focus on your grades and building good credit with your one card. Your expenses at this time are much less than what they will be after you graduate. Save your travel hacking for after you've signed a job contract.

Having a good credit score (the higher the better, but over 700 is a good number to aim for) will benefit you in the future, particularly when you want to purchase something you need a loan for. Keep in mind that credit cards are not free money, but most simply, a reflection of how financially responsible you are.

Planning For Your Future

College isn't an endgame, it is merely a stepping stone to get you where you want to be in five, 10, and 20 plus years from now. On that note, you should go through college in the mindset of using every resource to your advantage. While you are earning your degree, your job is to be a college student and your efforts should reflect that.

STEP 23: ESTABLISHING YOUR PERSONAL BRAND

By Nicole Booz

College is the perfect time to start building your personal brand. You are exposed to a myriad of opportunities and are creating valuable connections that will aid you as you build your career.

Establishing your brand, both in real life and online, is essential in building your professional reputation. It gives you control over how people perceive you and will enhance your credibility in the professional world.

How to build your brand:

1. **Ask yourself what traits you want to define you**. Examples include: dependable, hard-working, organized, or creative. If you're at a loss, ask trusted friends or family members to help you brainstorm.

2. **Ask yourself what field or career you want to work towards**. Maybe it is PR or psychology, maybe it is marketing or software development. Your career goals will change and your personal brand and mission statement will reflect that over time.

3. **Ask yourself what it is you are doing**. A fine answer for this is student or intern, but eventually you will be transitioning out of that role and into something else.

Once you've brainstormed these things, pull them together into a brief slogan for your brand. Use a descriptor, a field determinate, and a role you aim to fill. This is a quick snapshot to use on your blog, Twitter, LinkedIn, and résumé to let people know what they can expect from you.

How to implement your brand:

1. **Start a blog**. Having a blog will connect you to like-minded people, give you a space to share your thoughts and ideas, as

well as begin building your professional history. Use it as a space   to discuss career aspirations you have, research in your given field, techniques or concepts you have been learning in your classes. Keep it updated and post regularly, at least once a week. You can use your blog as a living résumé to keep track of the things you are doing to pursue your goals.

2. **Have a professional Twitter account**. Twitter is quickly turning into one of the most useful networking tools available. It's best to keep your professional and personal accounts separate. Link your blog to your Twitter account and your Twitter account to your blog to direct people there. Follow professionals in your field, as well as other bloggers, professors, researchers, and students. Share relevant links and thoughts at least once a day.

3. **Keep your LinkedIn and résumé updated**. When you apply to a job or internship, you better assume that they will be Google your name. Keeping all of your pages updated and professional will reflect that you are committed to your career and are up-to-date on what is happening in your industry. A knowledgeable employee is a valuable employee.

4. **Have a professional-type photo**. Understandably, a professional headshot may not be in the budget, but you still need a   photo where you are easily recognizable and isn't a selfie. Dress as you would if you were headed into work, and smile!

5. **Make it more difficult to find you on sites that you don't want employers to know about**. Again, employers will Google you. Your co-workers will Google you. As good practice to keep your personal and professional self separate, build a secondary online identity that does not link you to your real name. Consider a different spelling of your name, a nickname or only initials for accounts that don't align with your professional goals. Create a second email address to link these accounts to and do not use your professional photo with these accounts.

6. **Get a business card**. Seems crazy, right? You might be thinking it's a little early for that, but no. By the time you are a senior in college, chances are you are looking for a job and in the very least have sought out a few internships. Give your new connections the ability to find you online. It's a savvy way to share your name, blog link, Twitter handle, and LinkedIn account. People will know how to find you and are more likely to remember you this way.

Your professional persona will grow over time and your career goals will change as well. Your work will reflect that and so should your personal brand.

STEP 24: CREATING AN ONLINE PORTFOLIO
By Tynisha Ferguson

Creating an online portfolio is an excellent way to distinguish yourself in today's job market. No matter which career field or industry you are pursuing, online portfolios are a great way to share and showcase your work to future employers. Since you are taking time to gain relevant experience, allow your online portfolio to be your marketing tool.

However, simply having an online portfolio is not enough. You need to create an outstanding portfolio that not only showcases your abilities, but also displays your professional personality.

Some things to include in your portfolio include an "about me" page or a biography, samples of your best work, recommendations, references, a "contact me" page, a résumé, presentations, and even your thought process behind certain projects. Include anything that can display the professional quality of your work.

Websites[b] that we have found useful for creating professional portfolios are:

1. **WordPress**. WordPress is probably the most commonly used platform to create an online portfolio. It is relatively simple and it is free. With WordPress, there are endless themes – both free and paid, design options, widgets, and plugins to choose from to make your portfolio stand out.

2. **Behance**. The Behance network is also a great place to host your online portfolio. As an added bonus, it is also a social network where you can follow and connect with other creative professionals and employers.

3. **Wix**. For beginners looking to make a fast and easy professional looking online portfolio, Wix is great to try out because they offer over 280 professional looking templates. You can also create your own custom design. However, the downside to Wix is that once you commit to a template, you cannot change it.

4. **Clippings.me**. Specifically designed for writers, clippings.me allows writers and journalists to easily upload PDFs of their print writing samples and connect links to their online work. There is even space for a brief biography as well as links to your social media profiles.

5. **Weebly**. Easy to navigate, create, and edit, Weebly is an excellent option if you have minimal HTML or design skills. Unlike Wix, you can customize and edit your Weebly site as often as you like, and you can even build a blog directly on your site.

Be sure to highlight your best work and include an email address or phone number – no one can hire you if they can't contact you!

---

[b] This list of websites and the corresponding information were correct and up-to-date when this book was published.

Include links to your other social media sites as well so anyone browsing knows where else they can find you online.

We recommend personalizing your own domain name in the early stages of creating your portfolio. Most sites will charge you a flat fee each year, some monthly, to use your own domain name which you can purchase through sites such as NameCheap and GoDaddy.

STEP 25: HOW TO GET THE MOST FROM YOUR INTERNSHIPS
By Natalee Desotell, Dana Johnson & Abbygail Saddoy

It goes without saying that your goal when it comes to internships is to find one relevant to your field or career goals. However, you may not end up with the perfect or most appropriate internship for you.

Regardless, you can still find closely connected opportunities and experiences and turn them into résumé-worthy material.

Landing the Internship

1. **Do your research**. It's critical to know what internships are available. Even if you can't land a hands-on position, you should still make an effort to find an internship in a relevant field or office. Check with your school's career center, the local newspaper, internships.com, or internmatch.com. Pro-tip: Don't restrict yourself to specific companies. It takes many people filling many different roles to run a company - chances are you can find the experiences you are looking for in smaller or start-up companies.

2. **Clean up your paperwork**. Companies looking for interns don't have time to read your entire résumé and cover letter. Make sure it is up-to-date, highlights your previous experiences that make you the best person for the job, and double-check for typos and grammatical errors.

3. **Take advantage of other resources**. The internet isn't the only place to find an internship. Talk to your program's advisors, professors, and student organizations. Check message boards in coffee shops around campus, or information boards in hallways. As always, network. Make connections everywhere you go and opportunity will be sure to follow (see Step 26).

4. **Bring your A-game to the interview**. If you've made it to the coveted interview, congrats! Chances are not many people made it this far and now is the time you really need to stand out. Be present in your interview, answer questions honestly, prepare and practice answers beforehand. Have a few past experiences on hand that illustrate how you approached a problem and solved it. When your interviewer asks you about yourself - be honest, but don't over share. Make an effort to connect with the interviewer in some way. Did you both go to the same school? Were you both psychology majors? Did you both have an Australian Shepherd growing up? Be memorable in a good way.

During Your Internship

1. **Don't arrive with the attitude that you're above certain types of work**. There's a reason the stereotypical intern is one who spends their day juggling unreasonably complicated coffee orders. Hint: it's because that's what a lot of internships consist of, at least until you've paid your dues. If you maintain a positive attitude while performing menial tasks, though, you'll likely get more interesting jobs eventually.

2. **Dress the part**. Make sure you have a few important staples for your first few days, but it's best to do most of your shopping after you've had a chance to check out what the staff are wearing. No need to break the bank for internship duds, though; resale shops often have plenty of business casual selections to get you through.

3. **Network**! Treat everyone you meet–from the cleaning crew to the CEO–with respect. Everyone from the higher-ups to your fellow interns can be a great source for career advice and for finding out about other career-enhancing opportunities later on. You never know who might be able to help you get a job after graduation or willing to write you a letter of recommendation.

4. **Utilize your listening skills**. Make a strong effort to be educated about your company, your department, and the specific team you work for. Find out what projects your colleagues are working on, and show a genuine interest in them. Ask your supervisor questions about her role and responsibilities, and begin thinking about ways that your skills can be utilized on different projects.

5. Never underestimate the worth of asking questions. If you can show your coworkers that you have an interest in their assignments, they'll be more inclined to ask for your assistance. Better yet, if you've done your homework and can think of specific ways to help out, your co-workers will be able to recognize your willingness to contribute to meaningful tasks.

6. **Be efficient**. Whatever your tasks are, do them to the best of your ability, and do them efficiently. You have to organize the office supply cabinet? Make it spotless, and do it in half the time you're expected to. If your boss gives you a list of tasks to do for the day, finish them early and ask for more work. Sometimes you might finish your work early when your boss isn't around. Don't use this as an excuse to take some downtime. Instead, let your coworkers know that you're looking for some work and would love to help out however you can. This will show that you're motivated and honest, and it's a great way to network in the workplace.

After Your Internship

1. **Keep in touch**: Once you leave, a new intern will come in and take your place. Don't let your valuable contributions to the company get lost. Hopefully during your internship you made several meaningful connections with your coworkers and superiors. Send them an email every few weeks. We recommend sending a thank you card at the end of your internship to thank them for the time they took to help you and what you've gained from working there.

2. **Update your résumé as soon as possible**. The more time that passes, the more likely you are to forget things you did and skills you learned. Update your LinkedIn profile, too. Connect with anyone who worked in your office and ask them to endorse your skills.

STEP 25A: AFFORDING AN UNPAID INTERNSHIP
By Natalee Desotell

The fact that many internships are unpaid makes it difficult or impossible for low to middle-income students to afford them. When you're barely able to pay rent and stock your fridge, it's impossible to justify spending twelve or more hours per week working for free when you could be raking in at least $7.25 per hour flipping burgers. Unfortunately, unpaid internships perpetuate socioeconomic divisions by professionally disadvantaging students who simply can't take these unpaid opportunities.

If you've been offered an unpaid internship but don't know how you're going to make ends meet, there are a few options open to you.

First, several universities offer scholarships or stipends for students who are doing unpaid internships. Talk to your advisor to find out what's available.

Secondly, you can search for scholarships, grants or fellowships online; there are many organizations out there that give awards based on a specific field of study, merit or need.

Third, if you have already been interning for a year or more and have proven that you're worth keeping around, it's a good idea to be honest with your boss about your situation. They might be willing to work out a plan to start paying you for your valuable contributions to the office.

Additionally, consider finding a part-time unpaid internship to work alongside a paid part-time or full-time position. It isn't ideal, but you will still be able to pay your bills and get the experience from the internship.

STEP 25B: SIX EXPERIENCES TO BOOST YOUR RÉSUMÉ
By Nicole Booz

If you feel as though your résumé is lacking in relevant experience, seek out one or more of these activities and get involved:

1. A leadership role
2. Volunteer or service work
3. Clubs or organizations related to your major
4. Foreign language proficiency
5. Technical skills
6. Study abroad

STEP 26: THE INS AND OUTS OF NETWORKING
By Nicole Booz & Emily Field

If there is one thing you will hear over and over again, it's that networking is everything. When it really comes down to it, it isn't what you know, but who you know that makes all the difference.

We touched upon how to network with anyone earlier on (see Step 12), but now we are going to delve deeper into effective networking techniques that will help you establish mutually beneficial connections and make them last.

First of all, let's examine why you are failing at networking.

1. **You don't have your priorities in check.** If you are spending more time organizing your Pinterest boards than you are organizing your professional portfolio, your priorities aren't in the right place (unless organizing your Pinterest boards is the source of your paycheck, then we apologize and carry on). Dedicate time to connecting with individuals or professionals in your field. Make it a goal to end everyday with at least one new connection, whether they are in your field or not. Remember, all connections are valuable connections.

2. **You've checked all the right boxes, but haven't made any contacts.** The expectation that your résumé is going to speak for itself is a naive one to make. Yes, you had an internship with a PR firm, graduated with honors, were president of the physics club, stayed out of jail; it should be your turn to shine, right? Some of the most successful people have methodically and painfully worked their way up the ladder, so stop whining and get climbing. You have to contribute your time and support to make things happen for yourself.

3. **You rely on the internet to make connections for you.** We talk up online networking quite a bit, and in many ways, it has more pros than cons. However, it is not necessarily the best way to build an extensive network, particularly if you are location-dependent.

    For some reason we fear picking up the phone to talk to a real, live human being, or we hesitate meeting for coffee and would much rather Skype that interaction. Leaning on the technology crutch may appear easier than making face-to-face connections, but it can be ineffective in landing you the job.

When you submit that résumé into oblivion, wouldn't you like for someone to put a name to face? We may be New Age but some things are best done old school.

4. **You are too aggressive... or not aggressive enough.** When meeting a contact for the first time your approach is crucial. You do not want to come on too strong, but at the same time you want them to know you mean business. To avoid an overly aggressive image, lose the car salesman pitch. You are eager, talented, ambitious, have lots of ideas. We get it. Telling your story and telling your life story are two different things.

Instead, get to know the person, what they do, what their goals are, and work from there. Whether you are talking to the company big shot or the company janitor, appreciate his or her time spent talking to you. Have enthusiasm in your conversation and pay attention to details. By taking interest in your contact, you will make them feel valued and hopefully interested in continuing the relationship. Seize the opportunity to gain some new insights about their business or line of work.

5. **You haven't mastered the follow through.** You never know which people will be an important part of your career down the road, so it is vital to maintain relationships with your contacts. Follow up meetings with personal notes of gratitude and stay accountable of your promises to them. Both the size and quality of your network are important factors to take into account as well. You need more variety than a small group of close networks and more substance that a large group of unfamiliar acquaintances. Treat each business card you receive as paper gold. If the association don't immediately bring you an opportunity do not neglect the words of wisdom, and more importantly, don't burn the bridge. The world is pretty small, after all.

Did one or more of these areas resonate with you as a place of weakness? It's important to remember that networking is not about short-term gain. It's about learning, connecting, and growing as a professional. College students may feel that their student status leaves them at a disadvantage. But actually, quite the opposite is true. Seeds you plant today don't become flowers tomorrow, it takes time and nurture for them to grow and prosper. As a student, you have time and resources on your side.

Make an effort to talk to and connect with alumni from your university by attending alumni associated-hosted events. They are some of the best connections you could ever possibly make. By attending these events, you will be bumping elbows with well-connected people. Let them know your name, major, and areas of interest.

It is crucial to always share something that people will automatically associate with. Jane Smith won't know to email you with a research assistant opening if she doesn't know you are a third year psychology student with an interest in clinical research. People need to associate you with a specific interest if they are going to be able to help you.

STEP 26A: YOUR QUICK SPEECH: THE ELEVATOR PITCH
By Nicole Booz

This is the arguably the most important element of networking. You need to let others know who you are and what you do, and you need to do it effectively.

First you need to identify three things: what kind of job or position you are interested in, what your experience is, and what your best skills are. Write them down, and keep a running list. If you are having trouble brainstorming, ask friends and family to describe you.

Second, know what you are looking for. Your connections cannot help you if even you don't know what you are interested in. Is it an internship on your mind? A particular field? Certain responsibilities? A specific experience?

Narrow down the skills and experiences you already have under your belt that are the best fit for the position you are looking for. If you are unsure what qualifies, a good place to get inspiration is to look at current job listings for the job you want. The skills and experiences they list will be most important.

Once you've narrowed down the content, you will need to format your pitch. Start with who you are (including defining components, such as your current job title, major, or leadership role). Briefly describe a skill or two that you have learned and an example of how you have recently applied it (example: "I am a communications major with a focus in public relations. I recently completed an internship with our school newspaper where I developed and implemented a new strategy to increase our Twitter following by 200 percent."

End your speech with what you are looking for now. In this example, you may say, "I am searching for a position with a company to expand social campaign reach and impact, as well as strengthen connections with customers through social media."

Other helpful tips for developing your elevator pitch:

1. You will have to edit and refine your speech fairly often. Keeping a list of past accomplishments will help you do so quickly and in a pinch.
2. Tailor your pitch to the person you are talking to. Relate your experiences to them, their position, interests, and industry.
3. If the experience you have is niche-specific, eliminate technical words that might confuse the listener.
4. Be concise; your entire pitch should not exceed 60 seconds.

Think and speak in action verbs. This let's your target know how you accomplish things.

STEP 26B: MANAGING YOUR PROFESSIONAL TWITTER ACCOUNT
By Molly Berg

As more and more companies and professionals flock to Twitter, business connections and networks are rapidly developing.

1. Add a smiling, professional headshot and fill out your bio. Keep it short and sweet by including your current career goals or student status, a few interests, and the link to your website. Adapt your personal brand into 140 characters to keep consistent and recognizable across platforms.

2. Start connecting. Search for professionals in your industry by combing through the relevant hashtag. Once you've followed a few accounts, Twitter will begin recommending similar people to follow.

3. Produce your own content. Share your own work from your blog or portfolio occasionally, but also tweet other engaging content. Stay active by tweeting at least once per day. Pro-tip: You'll make more connections by tweeting more often. Make sure you tweet to individuals, thank them for following you, and to compliment or comment on their work.

4. The best way to network on Twitter? Participate in Twitter chats[21].

STEP 27: BUILDING AN ORGANIC MENTOR RELATIONSHIP
By Nicole Booz

College is the perfect time to initiate a mentor relationship. Your school may have a mentorship program to help connect your with an accomplished professional in your chosen field, and if not, you are still surrounded by knowledgeable and experienced individuals with whom you can build a relationship with.

Our tips for building an organic relationship with a mentor:

1. **Don't force it**. Organic means it develops naturally. It means you have common interests and career goals. Initiate a connection with a compliment or quick question. It may take a while to build a comfortable relationship, however, if they aren't interested in talking more with you, it's best to simply let it go.

2. **Mentors care about paying it forward**. You won't be proving outright why someone would make a good mentor for you. You should let them know how your goals intersect with theirs by complimenting or inquiring about their work first. If they see you as someone who has similar interests and values as they do, they will be more willing to talk to and connect with you.

3. **Ask questions**. Ask them about their career, projects they are working on, research they have done, or works they have published. You showing an interest in them will encourage them to show an interest in you.

4. **Cultivate the relationship**. You don't need to talk to your mentor daily or even weekly. But do make an effort to keep the connection strong. Send them an email with a relevant article you came across, ask them to have lunch or coffee with you, stop them in the hallway with a compliment.

5. **Say thank you**. When someone offers you advice, especially free advice, always follow it up with a thank you note. Send them an email or drop a note by their office (or mail it) within 24 hours of your chats, especially early on. If they know how much you appreciate them, they will be more willing to help you in the future.

Even if your relationship with your mentor started in a mentorship program, it will only be a beneficial relationship if you make it so. You won't be a good match for everyone and it will be detrimental to both of you to force the relationship.

Find and connect with someone who is a few years ahead of you in the field you want to go into. It may be a professor, someone from your internship, your boss, an older co-worker, a classmate, a teaching assistant, your resident assistant - possibilities for mentors are everyone.

Be open to connecting - a mentor relationship is about the facilitation of shared interests, knowledge, and goals.

TL; DR

We get it. You're busy and didn't have enough time to read this book cover to cover. We forgive you (only because we've been there, too). Just because we don't want you to miss out on all of the great advice we had for you, we put together this section.

1. Learn both hard skills and soft skills through your academics, internships, and extracurricular activities. See Step 2A.

2. You need to fine-tune your time management skills extremely early on in your college career. The sooner you learn your time-wasting triggers and can set a routine, the better off you will be. See Step 3.

3. Want good grades? Show up to class and engage. Come prepared. And always do the extra credit. Always. See Step 4.

4. Your syllabus is the most important tool you have for acing your classes. Familiarize yourself with it as soon as possible. Note the course objectives and what topics your professor thinks are most important, and then apply those concepts in your assignments as often as you can. See Step 4B.

5. Stumped at small talk topics? Ask your conversation partner about their job, classes, or the latest book they read. See Step 12B.

6. Avoid college money traps by shopping off campus whenever possible. Everything is more expensive on campus. See Step 19.

7. Your student loans may be necessary to fund your education, but picking up a part-time job could be the difference between $30k and $20k in student loan debt when you graduate. See Step 20.

8. Want to stand out from the crowd? Start a blog, connect with industry leaders on Twitter and LinkedIn, and be vocal. See Step 23.

9. Need a little something extra to add to your résumé? We recommend a volunteer trip, a shadowing position, experience with a foreign language, or a leadership role. See Step 25B.

10. The best people to network with? Alumni. See Step 26.

About GenTwenty

GenTwenty is an online lifestyle magazine where twenty-somethings get answers, advice, and a little encouragement about growing up and navigating the real world.

GenTwenty was founded in March 2013 with the passion to dispel myths surrounding Gen Y while providing support and reassurance to twenty-somethings everywhere.

Our twenty-something years of experience have taught us that life is about figuring it out as you go, and you are not alone. There are millions of your peers out there right now wondering the same things you are; who are feeling and experiencing the same things you are.

GenTwenty is the place for twenty-somethings to write about the issues that speak to them. Sharing our own personal experiences is an undeniably brilliant way of connecting with those around us. But, we also need advice. We need answers. We need encouragement. We need help sometimes too. And we also need to bask in the fact that we're all in this together, one year at a time.

ABOUT NICOLE BOOZ

Nicole is the Editor-in-Chief at GenTwenty. She graduated from the University of Maryland, College Park with a B.S. in Psychology. In her free time she enjoys exploring local markets, planning her next vacation, and reading any book she can get her hands on. Nicole hopes to connect others through ideas and shared experiences.

References

1. http://nces.ed.gov/fastfacts/display.asp?id=372

2. http://trends.collegeboard.org/college-pricing/figures-tables/average-published-undergraduate-charges-sector-2013-14

3. https://www.scholarships.com/resources/campus-life/college-costs/books-and-supplies/

4. http://www.pewsocialtrends.org/2014/02/11/chapter-1-education-and-economic-outcomes-among-the-young/

5. http://libertystreeteconomics.newyorkfed.org/2014/09/are-the-job-prospects-of-recent-college-graduates-improving.html#.VDhrUSldVy9

6. http://www.forbes.com/sites/halahtouryalai/2014/02/21/1-trillion-student-loan-problem-keeps-getting-worse/

7. http://calnewport.com/blog/2008/08/08/the-unconventional-scholar-dont-discuss-your-major-with-your-parents/

8. http://thechoice.blogs.nytimes.com/2013/04/29/does-the-college-major-matter-not-really/?_r=0

9. http://www.forbes.com/sites/susanadams/2013/10/11/the-10-skills-employers-most-want-in-20-something-employees/

10. https://www.scholarships.com/resources/campus-life/college-costs/books-and-supplies/

11. http://chronicle.com/article/EmployersPublic-Favor/141679/

12. http://collegelife.about.com/od/academiclife/g/Academic-Probation.htm

13. http://www.entrepreneur.com/article/227371

14. http://science.howstuffworks.com/life/exercise-happiness2.htm

15. http://content.time.com/time/magazine/article/0,9171,153672,00.html

16. http://adcaps.wsu.edu/alcohol101/blood-alcohol-chart/

17. http://www.abovetheinfluence.com/facts/drugsalcohol

18. http://www.drugfree.org/join-together/alcohol/combining-energy-drinks-with-alcohol-more-dangerous-than-drinking-alcohol-alone

19. http://www.nsvrc.org/saam/campus-resource-list#Stats

20. http://www.theglobeandmail.com/globe-debate/another-day-smarter-but-deeper-in-debt/article14157421/

21. See: http://gentwenty.com/5-twitter-chats-for-millennials/ and http://gentwenty.com/5-twitter-chats-millennials-part-2/

For an easily accessible list of these resources, visit gentwenty.com/college-success-references

www.ingramcontent.com/pod-product-compliance
Lightning Source LLC
La Vergne TN
LVHW011212080426
835508LV00007B/742